Richard Johnson

**The History of South America**

Containing the discoveries of Columbus, the conquest of Mexico and Peru, and

other transactions of the Spanish in the New World

Richard Johnson

**The History of South America**
*Containing the discoveries of Columbus, the conquest of Mexico and Peru, and other transactions of the Spanish in the New World*

ISBN/EAN: 9783337319250

Printed in Europe, USA, Canada, Australia, Japan

Cover: Foto ©ninafisch / pixelio.de

More available books at **www.hansebooks.com**

# THE HISTORY OF SOUTH AMERICA.

CONTAINING THE

Discoveries of Columbus,

THE

Conquest of Mexico and Peru,

AND THE

Other Transactions of the Spaniards

IN THE

NEW WORLD.

By the Rev. Mr. Cooper.

Embellished with Copper-plate Cuts.

LONDON,
Printed for E. Newbery, the Corner of St. Paul's Church-Yard, 1789.

# FRONTISPIECE.

*Navigation, Hope, & Fame, inviting Columbus to the Discovery of the New World.*

THE History of South America, like all other histories of newly discovered countries, has been so intervowen with fable, as in some measure to deter the youthful student from employing his time in the pursuit of *Trifles*; for in that light fabulous histories must generally be considered.

The Spanish Adventurers to the New World were mostly illiterate men, whose principal pursuits were gold and silver. On their return to their native state, their representations were guided by interest and vanity; and, ashamed of having made no observations on the rude arts, manufactures, and genius, of the people they had conquered, they fabricated stories the most wild, romantic and ridiculous,

## PREFACE.

to which the Spanish writers of those days gave a helping hand.

The literary world is undoubtedly much obliged to the labour, genius, and attention, of Dr. Robertson, whose extensive and polite connections enabled him to procure information for his History of America, which few other individuals could perhaps have obtained. We have therefore carefully consulted and followed that work, by the assistance of which we may venture to say, that we have now the pleasure of laying before our youthful Readers such an epitome of *The History of South America* as may by no means be considered as fabulous, but as founded on the most authentic materials and authorities.

## CHAP. I.

Origin of navigation.—Introduction of commerce.—Rude state of navigation among the ancients.—State of navigation and commerce among the Egyptians,—Phenicians,—Jews,—Carthaginians,—Greeks, and Romans.—Discoveries of the ancients by land.—Imperfect state of Geography among the ancients.—Commerce preserved in the Eastern empire.—Revival of commerce and navigation in Europe.—The crusades favourable to commerce.—The invention of the mariners compass.—First regular plan of discovery.—The Portuguese double Cape Non.—Discovery of Porto Santo,—Of Madeira.—The Portuguese double Cape Bojador, and advance within the tropics.—The Cape de Verd Islands and the Azores discovered.—The Portuguese cross the line,—They discover the Cape of Good Hope. . . P. 1.

## CHAP. II.

Birth and education of Columbus,—He enters into the service of the Portuguese,—He forms the idea of a new course to India,—He applies to the Genoese,—Then to Portugal, and afterwards to Spain,—Proposes his plan to Henry VIII. of England,—His treaty
with

## CONTENTS.

with Spain,—He sets sail on his voyage,—His crews are filled with alarms and apprehensions.—Land discovered.—First interview with the natives.—Columbus assumes the Title of admiral and vice-roy,—He discovers Cuba and Hispaniola.—Loses one of his ships,—His distresses,—Resolves to return to Europe,—Arrives in Spain, and receives the highest marks of honour.—He sets sail on his second voyage,—Builds the town of Isabella,—Discovers the island of Jamaica.—The Indians take arms against the Spaniards.—Columbus attacks and defeats them.—He taxes them.—Returns to Spain.—He sets sail a third time.—He discovers Trinidad.—Troubles at St. Domingo.—The Portuguese sail to the East-Indies by the way of the Cape of Good Hope.—From whom the name of AMERICA was given to the New World.—The Portuguese discover the Brasil.—Columbus sent in chains to Spain.—Is there set at liberty.—Sails a fourth time on discoveries.—Is wrecked on the coast of Jamaica.—Death of Columbus. 25

### CHAP. III.

State of the colony in Hispaniola.—New discoveries and settlements.—Diego Columbus appointed governor of Hispaniola.—

niola.—Sets sail for that island.—New discoveries made.—Attempts made to settle on the continent.—Discovery of Florida.—Discoveries of Balboa.—He enters the South Sea,—And returns.—Pedrarias Davila appointed governor of Darien.—His bad conduct.—Balboa publickly executed, through the treachery and intrigues of Pedrarias.—Further attempts at discovery.—The state of Hispaniola under Don Diego Columbus.—Death of Ferdinand, and accession of Charles the Fifth.—New discoveries made towards the West.—Discovery of Yucatan.—Are attacked by the Indians, and defeat them.—The Spaniards quit that place.—Arrive at Campeachy.—Meet with a defeat on landing to take in water, and are forced to return to Cuba.—Voyage of Juan de Grijalva.—He discovers New Spain.—Touches at Tabasco; and then at Guaxaca.—Lands on the isle of Sacrifices, and then touches at St. Juan de Ulua. . 51

CHAP. IV

Vast extent of the New World.—Its prodigious mountains.—Rivers and Lakes.—Temperature of the climate.—Its original rude state.—Its animals.—Insects and reptiles.—Birds.—Soil.—How was America first peopled?—

Character

## CONTENTS.

Character and condition of the original Americans.—The first discoverers of the New World mostly illiterate men.—The bodily constitution of the South Americans. — Their complexion. — Have small appetites.—None of them deformed.—State of their health and diseases.—Power and qualities of their minds.—The active efforts of their minds few and languid. — Domestic union.—The condition of the American women humiliating and miserable.—Parental affection and filial duty.—Mode of subsistence.—Fishing, hunting, and agriculture.—The Americans divided into small communities.—Had no notion of property.—Their method of carrying on war.—Their dress and ornaments.—Habitations.—Their arms—Domestic utensils and cookery.—Their canoes. — Ideas of Religion. — Their physicians, — Dancing, gaming, and drinking, their favourite amusements.—Destroy the aged and incurable.—Their general character. . . . . . 76

## CHAP. V.

Velasquez makes preparations for the invasion of New Spain.—Ferdinando Cortes undertakes the command of that expedition.—His forces.—Cortes sets sail with his little armament.
—Arrives

CONTENTS.

—Arrives in Mexico.—Rich prefents fent from Montezuma to Cortes.—Character of Montezuma.—Cortes refigns his commiffion, and is chofen by his officers and followers chief-juftice and captain-general of the new colony.—He proceeds to Zimpoalla. — From thence to Quiabiflan.—Builds a town there, and forms alliances.—Cortes deftroys his own fleet.—Advances into the country.—Concludes a peace with the Hafcalans. — Sets out for Mexico.—The Spaniards aftonifhed at the diftant view of that city.—Firft interview between Cortes and Montezuma.—Dangerous fituation of the Spaniards in Mexico.—Montezuma feized as a prifoner, and carried to the Spanifh quarters.—Montezuma's fon, and five of his officers, burnt alive, by order of Cortes.—The Mexican monarch acknowledges himfelf to be a vaffal of the king of Caftile.—A new Spanifh armament arrives at Mexico, fitted out by Velafquez to deftroy Cortes —Cortes attacks Narvaez in the night, defeats his forces, and takes him prifoner.—The greater part of the Spanifh prifoners enter into the fervice of Cortes.—The Mexicans take up arms againft the Spaniards.—Montezuma flain by his own people.—Cortes abandons the city of Mexico.—The Mexicans defeat him.—

Is

Is reduced almost to famine.—The battle of Otumba.—Cortes receives considerable reinforcements.—Builds and launches several brigantines on the lake.—The brigantines defeat the Mexican canoes on the lake.—Attacks the city of Mexico, Cortes defeated and wounded, forty of his men taken, and sacrificed to the god of war.—Cortes again attacks the city, and takes the emperor prisoner.—The Spaniards much disappointed in their expectations of the riches the conquest of this city would afford them.—Cruel treatment of the emperor—The whole province of Mexico subdued by the Spaniards.—The straits of Magellan discovered.—Death of Magellan.—Cortes appointed captain-general and governor of New Spain.—Sets out for the court of Castile.—The reception he meets with there.—Returns to New Spain, and discovers California.—Death of Cortes. . . . . . . 103

## CHAP. VI.

First attempts to discover Peru unsuccessful.—Pizarro, Almagro, and Luque, undertake that business.—Pizarro sets sail from Panama on his first expedition.—Experiences great hardships.—Discovers Peru.—The Spaniards are surprised at the riches and fertility of that country.—Return to Panama.—

## Contents.

Pizarro is sent to Spain, where he gets himself appointed captain-general, &c. of the new discoveries.—Pizarro sails on another expedition, and lands in Peru.—Commences hostilities.—Limits of the the Peruvian empire.—A civil war rages in Peru at the time of the arrival of the Spaniards.—Pizarro turns that circumstance to his advantage.—State of his forces.——Arrives at Caxamalca.——Treacherously seizes on the person of the Inca.—Massacre of the Peruvians.—Almagro arrives with reinforcements.—Division of the immense ransom of the Peruvian Inca.—The Inca put to death.—Pizarro leaves Caxamalca, and marches to Cuzco.—He takes possession of that capital, and seizes on immense treasures.—Pizarro sets out for Spain—His reception there.—Sets out on his return to Peru.—Settles differences there with his associate Almagro.—Pizarro builds the city of Lima.—Almagro marches towards Chili.—An insurrection in Peru.—The Peruvians besiege Cuzco.—Engage Almagro, and are defeated.—Civil war among the Spaniards.—Almagro defeated, tried, condemned, and executed.—Progress of the Spanish arms.—Chili conquered.——Treachery and ingratitude of Orellana.—Miserable condition of the followers of Pizarro, in consequence of that treachery.—

CONTENTS.

ry.—Francifco Pizarro murdered in his palace.—Almagro proclaimed governor of the city.—Vaca de Caftro arrives at Quito, and affumes the name of governor.—Difputes between him and Almagro.—The emperor reforms the government of his American dominions.—Sends over a vice-roy, who is killed in battle.—Pedro de la Gafca fent out as prefident of Peru.—Gonzalo Pizarro affumes the government, oppofes Gafca, is defeated, tried, and put to death.—Gafco fets out for Spain.—His reception there. . . . . . . . . . . 133

CONCLUSION.

Political inftitutions and national manners of the Mexicans and Peruvians.—Origin of the Mexican monarchy.—The city of Mexico, when founded.—Splendour and power of their monarchs.—Their wars.—Funeral rites.—Agriculture.—Temples, and other public buildings.—Religion of the Mexicans.—Peruvian antiquity doubtful.—Abfolute power of their Incas——The filver mines of Ptofi.——The Peruvian wars conducted with humanity.—Their improved ftate of agriculture.—Tafte in their buildings.—The Peruvians of an unwarlike spirit. . . . . . . . . . . 161

THE

# THE HISTORY OF SOUTH AMERICA.

## CHAP. I.

So nice and complicated are the arts of navigation and ship-building, that they require the ingenuity and experience of many succeeding ages, to bring them to any tolerable degree of perfection. The raft or canoe, which at first served to convey a savage over a river, that obstructed him in the chase, gave rise to the invention of constructing a vessel capable of carrying a number of people in safety to a distant coast. Many efforts were made, many experiments were tried, and much labour and invention employed, before this important undertaking was accomplished.

In proportion as the art of navigation encreased, men became more acquainted with each other, and a commercial intercourse commenced between remote nations. Men must have made some confiderable advancements towards civilization, before they acquired the idea of property, and ascertained it so perfectly, as to be acquainted with the most simple of all contracts, that of exchanging by barter one rude commodity for another. However, as soon as this important right was established, and every individual felt, that he had an exclusive title to possess or alienate whatever he had acquired by his own labour or dexterity, the wants and ingenuity of his nature suggested to him, a new method of encreasing his acquisitions and enjoyments, by disposing of what appeared to him superfluous, in order to procure what was necessary or desirable in the possession of others.

As navigation and commerce extended, so in course did the intercourse of remote nations. The ambition of conquest, or the necessity of procuring new settlements, were no longer the sole motives of visiting distant lands. The desire of gain became a new spur to activity, roused adventurers, and sent them out on long voyages, in the pursuit of countries, whose produce or want might encrease that circulation, which nourishes and gives vigour to commerce. Trade proved a great source of discovery, difcovery, it opened unknown feas, it penetrated into new regions, and contributed more than any other caufe, to bring men acquainted with the fituation, the nature, and commodities of the different regions of the earth.

The ftructure of the veffels ufed by the ancients was very rude and imperfect, and their method of working them on the ocean was very defective. Though the property of the magnet, by which it attracts iron, was well known to the ancients, its more important and amazing virtue of pointing to the poles had entirely efcaped their obfervation. Deftitute of this faithful guide, which now conducts the pilot with fo much certainty in the unbounded ocean, during the darknefs of night, or when the heavens are covered with clouds, the ancients had no other method of regulating their courfe than by obferving the fun and ftars. Their navigation was confequently uncertain and timid. They dared not even to quit fight of land, but crept along the coaft, expofed to all the dangers, and retarded by all the obftructions, unavoidable in holding fuch an aukward courfe. An incredible length of time was requifite for performing voyages, which are now finifhed in a fhort fpace. Even in the mildeft climates, and in feas the leaft tempeftuous, it was

only

only during the summer months that the ancients ventured out of their harbours, the remainder of the year being lost in inactivity.

The Egyptians, soon after the establishment of their monarchy, are reported to have commenced a trade between the Arabian Gulph, or Red Sea, and the western coast of the great Indian continent. The commodities, which they imported from the East were carried by land from the Arabian Gulph to the banks of the Nile, and conveyed down that river to the Mediterranean; but the fertile soil and mild climate of Egypt, producing all the necessaries and comforts of life, the Egyptians had no inducements to undertake long and hazardous voyages.

The Phenicians possessed a spirit more favourable to commerce and discovery than the Egyptians. They had not, like the natives of Egypt, any distinguishing peculiarity in their manners and institutions; they were not addicted to any singular and unsocial form of superstition, and could mingle with other nations without scruple or reluctance. The territory they possessed was neither large nor fertile, and commerce was the only source from which they could derive opulence or power. The trade, therefore, carried on by the Phenicians of Sidon and Tyre was more

extensive

extensive and enterprising than that of any state in the ancient world. In many of the places to which they resorted, they planted colonies, and communicated to the rude inhabitants some knowledge of their arts and improvements.

The Jews, encouraged by the riches they saw the Phenicians acquiring from commerce, seemed desirous to endeavour to partake of it. Solomon fitted out fleets, which under the direction of Phenician pilots, sailed from the Red Sea to Tarshish and Ophir; but the singular institution of the Jews, the observance of which was enjoined by their Divine Legislator, with an intention of preserving them a separate people, uninfected by idolatry, prevented their being numbered among the nations, which contributed to improve navigation, or to make any material or useful discoveries.

The Carthagenians caught the spirit of commerce from the Phenicians and Jews. The commonwealth of Carthage applied to trade and naval affairs with the greatest success. They extended their navigation chiefly towards the west and north, and visited not only all the coasts of Spain, but those of Gaul, and penetrated at last into Britain. They made considerable progress by land, into the interior provinces of Africa, traded with some of them,

them, and subjected others to their empire. They sailed along the western coast of that great continent, almost to the tropick of Cancer, and placed several colonies, in order to civilize the natives, and accustom them to commerce.

It is evident that the Phenicians, who instructed the Greeks in many useful arts and sciences, did not communicate to them that extensive knowledge of navigation, which they themselves possessed; nor did the Romans imbibe that commercial spirit and ardour for discovery, which distinguished their rivals the Carthagenians. Though Greece be almost encompassed by the sea, which formed many spacious bays and commodious harbours; though it be surrounded by a vast number of fertile islands, yet, nowithstanding such a favourable situation, which seemed to invite that ingenious people to apply themselves to navigation, it was long before this art attained any degree of perfection among them. Even at the time, when the Greeks engaged in the famous enterprize against Troy, their knowledge in naval affairs seems not to have been much improved. Their vessels were of inconsiderable burthen, and mostly without decks. These had only one mast, and they were strangers to the use of anchors. All their operations in sailing were clumsy and unskilful.

The

The expedition of Alexander the Great into the East, confiderably enlarged the fphere of navigation and of geographical knowledge among the Greeks. He founded a great city, which he called Alexandria, near one of the mouths of the river Nile, that by the Mediterranean fea, and the neighbourhood of the Arabian Gulf, it might command the trade both of the Eaft and Weft. This fituation was chofen with fuch difcernment, that Alexandria foon became the chief commercial city in the world.

The progrefs made by the Romans in navigation and difcovery, was ftill more inconfiderable than that of the Greeks. The genius of the Roman people, their military education, and the fpirit of their laws, concurred to difcourage them from commerce and naval affairs. It was the neceffity of oppofing a formidable rival, not the defire of extending trade, which firft prompted them to aim at maritime power.

As foon as the Romans acquired a tafte for the luxuries of the Eaft, the trade with India through Egypt was pufhed with new vigour, and carried on to greater extent. By frequenting the Indian continent, navigators became acquainted with the periodical courfe of the winds, which, in the ocean that feparates Africa from India.

India, blow with little variation during one half of the year from the east, and during the other half blow with equal steadiness from the west. Encouraged by this observation, they abandoned their ancient slow and dangerous course along the coast, and as soon as the western monsoon set in, took their departure from Ocelis, at the mouth of the Arabian Gulf, and stretched boldly across the ocean. The uniform direction of the wind, supplying the place of the compass, and rendering the guidance of the stars less necessary, conducted them to the port of Musiris, on the western shore of the Indian continent. There they took on board their cargo, and returning with the eastern monsoon, finished their voyage to the Arabian gulf within the year. This part of India, now known by the name of the Malabar coast, seems to have been the utmost limits of ancient navigation in that quarter of the globe.

The discovery of this new method of sailing to India, is the most considerable improvement in navigation made by the Romans during the continuance of their power. In ancient times, the knowledge of remote countries was more frequently acquired by land than by sea; and the Romans, from their particular dislike to maritime affairs, may be said to have
totally

totally neglected the latter, though a much more preferable way to make difcoveries, being more eafy and expeditious.

If we reject fabulous and obfcure accounts, if we clofely abide by the light and information of authentic hiftory, without giving way to the conjectures of fancy, or the dreams of etymologifts, we muft conclude, that the knowledge which the ancients had acquired of the habitable globe was very confined and fuperficial. In Europe, the extenfive provinces in the eaftern part of Germany were little known to them. They were almoft totally unacquainted with the vaft countries which are now fubject to the kings of Denmark, Sweden, Pruffia, Poland, and the Ruffian empire. The more barren regions, which ftretch within the arctic circle, were quite unexplored. In Africa, their refearches did not extend far beyond the provinces which border on the Mediterranean, and thofe fituated on the weftern fhore of the Arabian gulf. In Afia, they were unacquainted with all the fertile and delightful countries beyond the Ganges, which furnifh the moft valuable commodities for the European commerce with India; nor do they feem to have ever penetrated into thofe immenfe regions, occupied by the wandering tribes, which they called by the general name of
Scythians,

Scythians, and now possessed by Tartars of various denominations, and by the Asiatic Russian subjects.

But however imperfect or inaccurate the geographical knowledge which the Greeks and Romans had acquired may appear, in respect of the present improved state of that science, their progress in discovery will seem considerable, and the extent to which they carried navigation and commerce, must be considered as great, when compared with the ignorance of early times. Geography continued to improve under the Romans so long as they remained in their powerful state; but when the barbarians broke in upon them, the consequence of luxury and effeminacy, the sciences then dwindled, and discoveries ceased to be made.

Constantinople, after the destruction of the Roman empire, though often threatened by the fierce invaders, who spread desolation over the rest of Europe, was so fortunate as to escape their destructive rage. The knowledge of ancient arts and discoveries were preserved in that city, a taste for splendour and elegance still subsisted, the productions and luxuries of foreign countries were in request, and commerce continued to flourish in Constantinople, when it was almost extinct in every other part of Europe.

Much

Much about the same time, a gleam of light and knowledge broke in upon the East. The Arabians, having contracted some relish for the sciences of the people whose empire they had contributed to overturn, translated the books of several of the Greek philosophers into their own language. The study of geography in course became an early object of attention to the Arabians; but that acute and ingenious people cultivated chiefly the speculative and scientific parts of geography. In order to ascertain the figure and dimensions of our earth, they applied the principles of geometry, they had recourse to astronomical observations, and employed experiments and operations, which Europe, in more enlightened times, have eagerly adopted and imitated.

The calamities and desolation brought upon the western provinces of the Roman empire by its barbarous conquerors, by degrees were forgotten, and in some measure repaired. The rude tribes which settled there, acquiring insensibly some idea of regular government, and some relish for the functions and comforts of civil life, Europe awakened, in some degree, from its torpid and inactive state, the first symptoms of which were discerned in Italy. The acquisition of these roused industry, and gave motion and vigour to all

all the active powers of the human mind; foreign commerce revived, navigation was attended to, and great pains taken to improve it.

From that period, the commercial spirit of Italy became active and enterprising. Venice, Genoa, and Pisa, rose from inconsiderable towns, to be populous and wealthy cities; their naval power encreased, their vessels frequented not only all the ports in the Mediterranean, but venturing sometimes beyond the straits, visited the maritime towns of Spain, France, the Low Countries, and England.

While the cities of Italy were thus advancing in their career of improvement, an event happened, the most extraordinary perhaps in the history of mankind, which, instead of obstructing the commercial progress of the Italians, contributed to its encrease. The martial spirit of the Europeans, heightened and inflamed by religious zeal, prompted them to attempt the deliverance of the Holy Land from the dominion of Infidels. Vast armies, composed of all the nations in Europe, moved towards Asia on this strange enterprise. The Genoese, Pisans, and Venetians, furnished the transports to carry them thither, and supplied them with provisions and military stores. Besides the immense sums which they received on this account, they
obtained

obtained commercial privileges and establishments. From thefe fources prodigious wealth flowed into the cities above mentioned. This was accompanied with a proportional encreafe of power, and by the end of the Holy War, Venice, in particular, became a great maritime ftate, poffeffing an extenfive commerce and ample territories.

Communications being thus opened between Europe and the weftern provinces of Afia, feveral perfons were encouraged to advance far beyond the countries, in which the crufaders carried on their operations, and to travel by land into the more remote and opulent regions of the Eaft. The wild fanaticifms, which feem at that period to have mingled in all the fchemes of individuals, no lefs than in all the councils of nations, firft incited men to enter upon thefe long and dangerous excurfions. They were afterwards undertaken from profpects of commercial advantage, or from motives of mere curiofity.

In the midft of this rifing defire for difcovery, a very fortunate event took place, which contributed more than all the efforts and ingenuity of preceding ages, to improve and extend navigation. That wonderful property of the magnet, by which it communicates fuch virtue to a needle or slender rod of iron, as to point towards the poles of the earth, was happily discovered. The use which might be made of this in directing navigation, was immediately perceived. From hence, that most valuable, but now familiar instrument, the mariners compass, was formed. As soon as navigators found by means of this, that at all seasons, and in every place, they could discover the North and South with so much ease and accuracy, it became no longer necessary to depend merely on the light of the stars, and the observation of the sea-coast. They gradually abandoned their ancient timid and lingring course along the shore, launched boldly into the ocean, and relying on this new guide, could steer in the darkest night, and under the most cloudy sky, with a security and precision hitherto unknown. The compass may be said to have opened to man the dominion of the sea, and to have put him in full possession of the earth, by enabling him to visit every part of it.

About the year 1365, Providence seemed to have decreed, that at this period men were to pass the limits within which they had been so long confined, and open to themselves a more ample field, wherein to display their talents, their enterprise, and courage. The first considerable efforts towards this were not made by any of the
more

more powerful states of Europe, or by those who had applied to navigation with the greatest assiduity and success. The glory of taking the lead in this bold attempt was reserved for the Portuguese, whose kingdom was the smallest and least powerful of any in Europe. As the attempts of the Portuguese to acquire the knowledge of those parts of the globe, with which mankind were then unacquainted, not only improved and extended the art of navigation, but roused such a spirit of curiosity and enterpize, as led to the discovery of the New World, of which we are presently to give the history.

Various circumstances urged the Portuguese to exert their activity in this new direction, and enabled them to accomplish undertakings apparently superior to the natural force of their monarchy. John I. king of Portugal, surnamed the Bastard, having obtained secure possession of the crown, in the year 1411, soon perceived, that it would be impossible to preserve public order, or domestic tranquility, without finding some employment for the restless spirit of his subjects. With this view, he assembled a numerous fleet at Lisbon, composed of all the ships he could fit out in his own kingdom, and of many hired from foreigners. This great armament, fitted out in 1412, was destined to attack the Moors settled on the coast of Barbary. While the fleet was equipping, a few vessels were appointed to sail along the western shore of Africa, bounded by the Atlantic ocean, and to discover the unknown countries situated there.

The peculiar situation of Portugal was an invitation to this new undertaking, and the genius of the age being favourable to the execution of it, it proved successful. The vessels sent on the discovery doubled the formidable Cape Non, which had terminated the progress of former navigators, and proceeded one hundred and sixty miles beyond it, to Cape Bojador. As its rocky cliffs, which stretched a considerable way into the Atlantic, appeared more dreadful than the promontory they had passed, the Portuguese commander was afraid to attempt to sail round it, but returned to Lisbon, more satisfied with having advanced so far, than ashamed of not having gone farther.

Though this voyage was in itself inconsiderable, yet it encreased the passion for discovery, which began to shew itself in Portugal. The fortunate issue of the king's expedition against the Moors of Barbary, added strength to that spirit in the nation, and pushed it on to new undertakings. In order to render these successful, it was necessary, that they should be

conducted

conducted by a perſon, who poſſeſſed abilities capable of diſcerning what was attainable, who enjoyed leiſure to form a regular ſyſtem for proſecuting diſcovery, and who was animated with ardour, that would perſevere in ſpite of obſtacles and repulſes. Happily for Portugal, ſhe found all theſe qualities in Henry duke of Viſeo, the fourth ſon of king John. That prince, in his early youth, having accompanied his father in his expedition to Barbary, diſtinguiſhed himſelf by many deeds of valour. To the martial ſpirit, which was the characteriſtic of every man of noble birth at that period, he added all the accompliſhments of a more enlightened and poliſhed age. He cultivated the arts and ſciences, which were then little known, and deſpiſed by perſons of his exalted ſituation. He was particularly fond of the ſtudy of geography, and he early acquired ſuch a knowledge of the habitable globe, as diſcovered the great probability of finding new and opulent countries, by ſailing along the coaſt of Africa.

The commencement of every new undertaking is uſually attended with trifling ſucceſs. In the year 1418, he fitted out a ſingle ſhip, and gave the command of it to two gentlemen of his houſehold, who offered themſelves as volunteers to conduct the enterpriſe. He inſtructed them to double

double Cape Bojador, and thence to steer towards the south. They held their course along the shore, the mode of navigation which still prevailed, when a sudden squall of wind arose, which drove them out to sea, and, when they expected every moment to perish, it blew them on an unknown island, which, from their happy escape, they named Porto Santo. They instantly returned to Portugal with the news of their discovery, and were received by Henry with the applause and honour due to fortunate adventurers.

The next year Henry sent out three ships under the same commanders, in order to make a settlement in Porto Santo. From this island they observed towards the south a fixed spot in the horizon, like a small black cloud. They were, by degrees, led to conjecture it might be land, and steering towards it, they arrived at a considerable island, uninhabited and covered with wood, which on that account they called Madeira. As it was Henry's principal object to render his discoveries useful to his country, he immediately equipped a fleet to carry a colony of Portuguese to these islands. He took care that they should be furnished not only with the seeds, plants, and domestic animals, common in Europe; but, as he foresaw that the warmth of the climate, and fertility of the soil,

would

would prove favourable to the rearing of other productions, he procured flips of the vine from the ifland of Cyprus, the rich wines of which were then in great requeft, and plants of the fugar cane from Sicily, into which it had been lately introduced. Thefe throve fo profperoufly in this new country, that the advantage of their culture was immediately perceived, and the fugar and wine of Madeira foon became confiderable articles of commerce, from which the Portuguefe derived great advantage.

Thefe important fucceffes gave a fpur to the fpirit of difcovery, and induced the Portuguefe, inftead of fervilely creeping along the coaft, to venture into the open fea. They doubled Cape Bojador, in 1433, and advanced within the tropics. In the courfe of a few years, they difcovered the river Senegal, and all the coaft extending from Cape Blanco to Cape de Verde.

The Portuguefe had hitherto been guided in their difcoveries, or encouraged to attempt them, by the light and information they received from the works of the ancient mathematicians and geographers; but, when they began to enter the torid zone, the notions which prevailed among the ancients, that the heat was there fo intenfe as to render it infupportable, deterred them, for fome time, from proceeding. However,

ever, notwithstanding these unfavourable appearances, in 1449 the Portuguese discovered the Cape de Verde islands, which lie off the promontory of that name, and soon after the isles called Azores. As the former of these are above three hundred miles from the African coast, and the latter nine hundred miles from any continent, it is evident, that the Portuguese had made great advances in the art of navigation.

The passion for discoveries received an unfortunate check by the death of prince Henry, whose superior knowledge had hitherto directed all the operations of the discoverers, and whose patronage had encouraged and protected them. However, notwithstanding all the advantages they derived from hence, the Portuguese, during his life, did not advance, in their utmost progress towards the south, within five degrees of the equinoctial line; and, after their continued exertions for half a century, hardly fifteen hundred miles of the coast of Africa were discovered.

The Portuguese, in 1471, ventured to cross the line, and, to their astonishment, found that region of the torid zone, which was supposed to be scorched with intolerable heat, to be habitable, populous, and fertile.

Under

Under the direction of John II. in 1484, a powerful fleet was fitted out, which advanced above fifteen hundred miles beyond the line, and the Portuguese, for the first time, beheld a new heaven, and observed the stars of another hemisphere.

By their constant intercourse with the people of Africa, they gradually acquired some knowledge of those parts of that country, which they had not visited. The information they received from the natives, added to what they had observed in their own voyages, began to open prospects of a more extensive nature. They found, as they proceeded southward, that the continent of Africa, instead of extending in breadth, according to the doctrine of Ptolemy, appeared sensibly to contract itself, and to bend towards the East. This induced them to give credit to the accounts of the ancient Phenician voyages round Africa, which had long been considered as fabulous, and gave them reason to hope, that by following the same route, they might arrive at the East Indies, and engross that commerce, which had so long contributed to enrich other powers.

In 1486, the conduct of a voyage for this purpose, the most dangerous and difficult the Portuguese had ever embarked in, was entrusted to Bartholomew Diaz, who
stretched

stretched boldly towards the South, and proceeding beyond the utmost limits to which his countrymen had hitherto advanced, discovered near a thousand miles of a new country. Neither the combined powers of violent tempests, and the frequent mutinies of his crew, nor even the calamities of famine, which he suffered from loosing his store-ship, could deter him from the pursuit of his grand object. In spite of all, he at last discovered that lofty promontory, which bounds Africa to the South; but he did nothing more than discover it. The violence of the winds, the shattered condition of his ships, and the turbulent spirit of his sailors, compelled him to return after a voyage of sixteen months. The King of Portugal, as he now entertained no doubt of having found the long desired route to India, gave this promontory the name of The Cape of Good Hope.

These sanguine ideas of success were strengthened by the intelligence the King received over land, in consequence of his embassy to Abyssinia. Covillam and Payva, by the King's instructions, had repaired to Grand Cairo. From this city, they travelled in company with a caravan of Egyptian merchants, and embarking on the Red Sea, arrived at Arden in Arabia. There they separated: Payva sailed directly

rectly towards Abyssinia; Covillam embarked for the East Indeis, and having visited Calecut, Goa, and other cities of the Malabar coast, returned to Sofala, on the east side of Africa, and thence to Grand Cairo, which Payva and he had fixed upon as their place of meeting. The former, however, was unfortunately and cruelly murdered in Abyssinia; but Covillam found at Cairo two Portugese Jews, whom the King of Portugal had dispatched after them, in order to receive an account of their proceedings, and to communicate to them new instructions. By one of these Jews, Covillam transmitted to Portugal a journal of his proceedings by sea and land, his remarks upon the trade of India, together with exact maps of the coasts on which he had touched; and from what he himself had observed, as well as from the information of skilful seamen in different countries, he concluded, that by sailing round Africa, a passage might be found to the East Indies. The happy coincidence of Covillam's report and opinion with the discoveries lately made by Diaz, left hardly any shadow of doubt with respect to the possibility of sailing from Europe to India. However, the vast length of the voyage, and the furious storms, which Diaz had encountered near the Cape of Good Hope, alarmed and intimidated

timidated the Portuguese to such a degree, although they were become adventurous and skilful mariners, that some time was requisite to prepare their minds for this dangerous and extraordinary voyage.

---

*Memorable Events recorded in this Chapter.*

Introduction of commercial pursuits.

Imperfections of navigation among the ancients.

Navigation and commerce of the Egyptians, Phenicians, Jews, Carthaginians, Greeks, and Romans.

The first regular plan of discovery formed by the Portuguese.

The use of the mariners compass discovered about 1322.

The Portuguese double Cape Bojador about the year 1412.

Attempts to discover a new route to the East Indies.

Voyage of Bartholomew Diaz, in 1486, who penetrated as far as the Cape of Good Hope.

## CHAP. II.

CHRISTOPHER COLUMBUS, a subject of the republic of Genoa, was among the foremost of those foreigners, whom the fame of the discoveries made by the Portuguese had allured into their service. Though neither the time nor place of his birth are certainly known, yet it is on all hands agreed, that he was descended from an honourable family reduced to indigence by misfortunes. As his ancestors were accustomed to a seafaring life, Columbus became naturally fond of it himself, and very early discovered those talents for that profession, which plainly indicated the great man he was one day to be. He applied with uncommon ardour to the study of the Latin tongue, geography, astronomy, and the art of drawing. Thus qualified, in 1461, at the age of fourteen, he went to sea, and began his career on that element, which conducted him to so much glory.

In 1467, he repaired to Lisbon, where many of his countrymen were settled. They soon conceived such a favourable opinion of his merit and talents, that they warmly solicited him to remain in their kingdom, where his naval skill and experience

perience could not fail of rendering him conspicuous.

To find out a passage by sea to the East Indies, was the great object in view at that period. From the time that the Portuguese doubled Cape de Verde, this was the point at which they aimed in all their navigations. The tediousness of the course, which the Portuguese were pursuing, naturally led Columbus to consider, whether a shorter and more direct passage to the East Indies, than that projected by sailing round the African continent, might not be found out. After revolving long and seriously every circumstance suggested by his superior knowledge in the theory, as well as practice of navigation, after comparing attentively the observations of modern pilots, with the hints and conjectures of ancient authors, he at last concluded, that by sailing directly towards the West, across the Atlantic ocean, new countries, which probably formed a part of the vast continent of India, must infallibly be discovered.

Filled with these ideas, he laid his scheme before the senate of Genoa, and making his country the first tender of his service, offered to sail under the banners of the republic, in quest of the new regions he expected to discover; but they inconsiderately rejected his proposal, as the dream

of

of a chimerical projector. He then submitted his plan to the Portuguese, who endeavoured to rob him of the honour, by sending another person privately to pursue the same track proposed by him; but the pilot, chosen to execute Columbus's plan, had neither the genius nor the fortitude of its author. Contrary winds arose, no sight of approaching land appeared, his courage failed, and he returned to Lisbon, execrating a plan, which he had not abilities to execute.

Columbus no sooner discovered this dishonorable treatment, than he instantly quitted Portugal in disgust, and repaired to Spain about the close of the year 1484. Here he resolved to propose it in person to Ferdinand and Isabella, who at that time governed the united kingdoms of Castile and Arragon. He also sent his brother to England, to propose his plan to Henry VIII.

After a long succession of mortifying circumstances and disappointments, Isabella was persuaded to send for Columbus to court. The cordial reception he there met with from the queen, together with the near prospect of setting out upon that voyage, which had so long been the object of his thoughts and wishes, soon effaced the remembrance of all that he had suffered in Spain, during eight tedious years of
solicitation

solicitation and suspence. The negociation now went forward rapidly, and a treaty with Columbus was signed on the 17th of April, 1492.

The chief articles of it were, 1. Ferdinand and Isabella, as sovereigns of the ocean, constituted Columbus their high admiral in all the seas, islands, and continents, which should be discovered by his industry; and stipulated, that he and his heirs should enjoy this office, with the same powers and prerogatives, which belonged to the high admiral of Castile, within the limits of his jurisdiction. 2. They appointed Columbus their viceroy in all the islands and continents which he should discover; but if, for the better administration of affairs, it should hereafter be necessary to establish a separate governor in any of those countries, they authorised Columbus to name three persons, of whom they would choose one for that office; and the dignity of viceroy, with all its immunities, was likewise to be hereditary in the family of Columbus. 3. They granted to Columbus and his heirs, for ever, the tenth of the free profits accruing from the productions and commerce of the countries which he should discover. 4. They declared, that if any controversy or law-suit should arise with respect to any mercantile transaction in the

the countries which should be discovered, it should be determined by the sole authority of Columbus, or of judges to be appointed by him. 5. They permitted Columbus to advance one eight part of what should be expended in preparing for the expedition, and in carrying on commerce with the countries which he should discover, and entitle him, in return, to an eighth part of the profit.

Ferdinand, though his name appears conjoined with that of Isabella in this transaction, refused to take any part in it as King of Arragon, his distrust of Columbus being very violent.

After all the efforts of Isabella and Columbus, the armament was not suitable, either to the dignity of the power who equipped it, or to the importance of the service to which it was destined. It consisted of three vessels. The largest, a ship of no considerable burden, was commanded by Columbus, as admiral, who gave it the name of Santa Maria. Of the second, called the Pinta, Martin Pinzon was captain, and his brother Francis pilot. The third, named the Nigna, was under the command of Vincent Yanez Pinzon. These two were light vessels, hardly superior in burden or force to large boats. The sum employed in the whole of this equipment did not exceed 4000 l.

On the 3d day of August, 1492, Columbus set sail, a little before sun-rise, in presence of a vast crowd of spectators, who sent up their supplications to heaven for the prosperous issue of the voyage, which they wished rather than expected. Columbus steered directly for the Canary Islands, from whence he departed on the 6th of September. In the short run to the Canaries, the ships were found to be so crazy and ill appointed, as to be very improper for a navigation, which was expected to be both long and dangerous.

Columbus, on leaving the Canaries, held his course due west, left immediately the usual track of navigation, and stretched into unfrequented and unknown seas. By the 14th of September, the fleet was about two hundred leagues to the West of the Canary islands, at a greater distance from land than any Spaniard had been before that time. Columbus early discovered from the spirit of his followers, that he must prepare to struggle, not only with the unavoidable difficulties, which might be expected from the nature of his undertaking, but with such as were likely to arise from the ignorance and timidity of the people under his command. All the art and address he was master of was hardly sufficient to quell the mutinous disposition of his sailors, who grew the more turbulent,

bulent, in proportion as their diftance encreafed from home.

On the 11th of October, Columbus was fo confident of being near land, that he ordered the fails to be furled, and the fhips to lie by, keeping ftrict watch, left they fhould be driven on fhore in the night. During this interval of fufpence and expectation, no man fhut his eyes, all kept upon deck, gazing intently towards that quarter where they expected to difcover the land, which had been fo long the object of their wifhes. A little after midnight, the joyful found of *land! land!* was heard from the Pinta, which kept always a-head of the other fhips; but, having been fo often deceived by fallacious appearances, every man was now become flow of belief, and waited, in all the anguifh of uncertainty and impatience, for the return of day.

On the 12th of October, as foon as morning dawned, all doubts and fears were difpelled. From every fhip an ifland was feen about two leagues to the North, whofe flat and verdant fields, well ftored with wood, and watered with many rivulets, prefented the afpect of a delightful country. The crew of the Pinta inftantly began the *Te Deum*, as a hymn of thankfgiving to God, and were joined by thofe of the other fhips, with tears of joy

and

and transports of congratulation. They then on their knees begged pardon of Columbus for the mutinous spirit they had shewn, acknowledged his superior abilities, and promised implicit obedience to his will in future.

The boats being manned and armed as soon as the sun arose, they rowed towards the island with their colours displayed, warlike music, and other martial pomp. As they approached the coast, they saw it covered with a multitude of people, whom the novelty of the spectacle had drawn together, whose attitudes and gestures expressed wonder and astonishment at the strange objects before them. He landed in a rich dress, with a sword in his hand. His men followed, and kneeling down, they all kissed the ground which they had so long desired to see. They then took solemn possession of the country for the crown of Castile and Leon.

The dress of the Spaniards, the whiteness of their skins, their beards, their arms, appeared strange and surprising to the natives. The vast machines in which they had traversed the ocean, that seemed to move upon the water with wings, and uttered a dreadful sound resembling thunder, accompanied with lightning and smoke, struck them with such teror, that they began to consider them as children of
the

the Sun, who had defcended to vifit mortals here below.

The Spaniards were no lefs furprifed at the novelty of their fituation. Every herb, fhrub, and tree, was different from thofe which flourifhed in Europe. The inhabitants appeared in the fimple innocence of nature, entirely naked. Their black hair, long and uncurled, floated upon their fhoulders, or was bound in treffes round their heads. They had no beards, and every part of their bodies was perfectly fmooth. Their complexion was of a dufky copper colour, their features fingular, rather than difagreeable, and their afpect gentle and timid. They were fhy at firft through fear, but foon became familiar with the Spaniards, and with tranfports of joy received from them hawks-bells, glafs beads, or other baubles, in return for which they gave fuch provifions as they had, and fome cotton yarn, the only commodity of value that they could produce. Thus in the firft interview between the inhabitants of the new and old worlds, every thing was conducted amicably, and to their mutual fatisfaction.

Columbus now affumed the title and authority of admiral and viceroy, and called the ifland he had difcovered San Salvador. It is one of that large clufter of iflands called the Lucaya or Bahama ifles. It is
fituated

situated above 3000 miles to the west of Gomera, from which the squadron took its departure, and only four degrees to the south of it.

It soon appeared evident to Columbus that this was but a poor place, and consequently not the object of his pursuit. But, conformably to his theory concerning the discovery of those regions of Asia, which stretched towards the east, he concluded that San Salvador was one of the isles, which geographers described as situated in the vast ocean adjacent to India; but he was herein mistaken. Having observed, that most of the people whom he had seen wore small plates of gold, by way of ornament, in their nostrils, he eagerly enquired where they got that precious metal. They pointed towards the south, and made him comprehend by signs, that gold abounded in countries situated in that quarter.

In consequence of this intelligence, he sailed to the southward, and saw several Islands. He touched at those of the largest, on which he bestowed the names of St. Mary, Fernandina, and Isabella; but, as all his enquiries were after gold, and none of them produced any, he made no stay in any of them. He afterwards discovered Cuba, and soon after fell in with Hispaniola.

Columbus,

Columbus, ſtill intent on diſcovering the mines which yielded gold, ſailed from hence on the 24th of December, 1492. The great variety of buſineſs in which he was engaged having prevented Columbus from taking any ſleep for two days, he retired at midnight, in order to take ſome repoſe, having committed the helm to the pilot, with ſtrict injunction not to quit it for a moment. The pilot, dreading no danger, careleſſly left the helm to an unexperienced cabin-boy, and the ſhip, carried away by a current, was daſhed againſt a rock. The violence of the ſhock awakened Columbus. He ran up to the deck, where all was confuſion and deſpair, he alone retaining preſence of mind. However, all his endeavours were in vain; the veſſel opened near the keel, and filled ſo faſt with water that its loſs was inevitable. The boats from the Nigna ſaved the crew, and the natives in their canoes did every thing in their power to ſerve them, by whoſe aſſiſtance they ſaved almoſt every thing that was valuable.

The diſtreſs of Columbus was at this time very great. The Pinta had ſailed away from him, and he ſuſpected was treacherouſly gone to Europe. There remained but one veſſel, and that the ſmalleſt and moſt crazy of the ſquadron, to traverſe ſuch a vaſt ocean, and carry ſo many men back to Europe. He reſolved therefore to

leave

leave a part of his crew on the island, that, by residing there, they might learn the language of the natives, study their dispositions, search for mines, and prepare for the commodious settlement of the colony, with which he proposed to return. Having settled this business with his men and the natives, he built a fort, and placed in it the guns saved out of his own ship. He appointed thirty-eight of his people to remain on the island, under the command Diego de Arada, and furnished them with every thing requisite for the subsistance or defence of the infant colony.

Having thus settled matters, he left Navidad on the 4th of January, 1493, and stretching towards the east, discovered and gave names to most of the harbours on the northern coast of the island. On the 6th he decried the Pinta, and soon came up with her, after an absence of six weeks. Pinzon endeavoured to justify his conduct, and though Columbus was by no means satisfied in his own mind, yet he thought it prudent to dissemble at present, and accordingly received him again into favour. Pinzon, during his abscence from the admiral, had visited several harbours in the island, had acquired some gold by traffic with the natives, but had made no discovery of any importance.

Columbus,

Columbus now found it necessary, from the condition of his ships, and the temper of his men, to return to Europe. Accordingly, on the 16th of January, he directed his course towards the north-east, and soon lost sight of land. The voyage was prosperous to the 14th of February, when he was ovetaken by so violent a storm, that all hopes of surviving it were given up. At length Providence interposed to save a life reserved for other purposes; and, after experiencing a second storm almost as dreadful as the first, he arrived at the Azores, then Lisbon, and reached Spain on the 15th of March, in the port of Palos, seven months and eleven days from the time when he set out from thence upon his voyage.

Columbus was received, on his landing, with all the honours due to his great abilities; and Ferdinand and Isabella were no less astonished than delighted with this unexpected event. Every mark of honour, that gratitude or admiration could suggest, was conferred upon Columbus. Letters patent were issued, confirming to him and his heirs all the previleges contained in the capitulation concluded at Santa Fé; his family was enobled, and the king, queen, and courtiers, treated him as a person of the highest rank. But what pleased him most was an order to equip, without delay, an armament of such force, as might enable him

him not only to take possession of the countries he had already discovered, but to go in search of those more opulent regions, which he still confidently expected to find.

Cautious as Ferdinand was, and averse to every thing new and adventurous, preparations for a second expedition were carried on with a rapidity unusual in Spain, and to an extent that would be deemed not inconsiderable in the present age. The fleet consisted of seventeen ships, some of which were of good burthen. It had on board 1500 persons, among whom were many of noble families, who had served in honourable stations.

Every thing being ready, Columbus set sail from the bay of Cadiz on the 25th of September, 1493, and arrived at Hispaniola on the 22d of November. When he appeared off Navidad, from the station in which he had left the thirty-eight men under the command of Arada, he was astonished that none of them appeared, and expected every moment to see them running with transports of joy to welcome their countrymen. But he soon found, that the imprudent and licentious behaviour of his men had roused the resentment of the natives, who at last destroyed them all and burned their fort.

He then traced out the plan of a town in a large plain, near a spacious bay, and obliged every person to put his hand to a
work,

work, on which their common safety depended. This rising city, the first that the Europeans founded in the New World, he named Isabella, in honour of his patroness the queen of Castile.

His followers loudly complained of being obliged to turn builders, where they expected to meet with riches and luxuries. He therefore found it necessary to proceed in quest of those golden shadows. Having settled every thing respecting the government of the new colony in his absence, he weighed anchor on the 24th of April, 1494, with one ship and two small barks under his command. During a tedious voyage of full five months, he had a trial of almost all the numerous hardships, to which persons of his profession are exposed, without making any discovery of importance, except the island of Jamaica.

On his return to Hispaniola, he met with his brother Batholomew at Isabella, after an absence of near thirteen years, which gave him inexpressible joy. He could not have arrived more seasonably, as the Spaniards were not only threatened with famine, but even with an insurrection of the natives, owing to the shameful liberties the new settlers took with the women and property of the Indians, who united their forces to drive these formidable invaders from the settlements, of which they had violently taken possession.

On the 24th of March, Columbus took the field with his little army, which consisted only of 200 foot, twenty horse, and twenty large dogs; and how strange soever it may seem, to mention the last as composing part of a military force, they were not perhaps the least formidable and destructive of the whole, when employed against naked and timid Indians. If we may believe the Spanish historians, the Indian army amounted to 100,000 men; but they were ignorant of the arts of war, and had nothing but clubs and arrows for their defence. Columbus attacked them during the night, and obtained an easy and bloody victory. Many were killed, more taken prisoners, and reduced to servitude; and so thoroughly were the rest intimidated, that they abandoned themselves to despair, considering their enemies as invincible.

Columbus employed several months in marching through the island, and in subjecting it to the Spanish government, without meeting with any opposition. He imposed a tribute upon all the inhabitants above fourteen years of age. Each person who lived in those districts where gold was found, was obliged to pay quarterly as much gold-dust as filled a hawk's bell; from those in other parts of the country, twenty pounds of cotton were demanded.

This

This was the first regular taxation of the Indians, and served as a precedent for exactions, still more exorbitant. Such an imposition was extremely contrary to those maxims which Columbus had hitherto inculcated, with respect to the mode of treating them.

The condition of the Indians became insupportable, and they endeavoured to starve the Spaniards, by destroying all the produce of the earth, and then retired to the mountains. This reduced the Spaniards to extreme want; but they received such seasonable supplies of provisions from Europe, and found so many resources in their ingenuity and industry, that they suffered no great loss of men.

Columbus finding he had many enemies in the court of Spain, resolved to return home in order to justify himself, leaving his brother Bartholomew as lieutenant-governor, and Francis Roldon chief justice. He was received at court, on his arrival, with so many marks of approbation, after having perfectly cleared up his conduct, as made his enemies ashamed of themselves, and it was resolved to send him on discoveries a third time.

After innumerable disappointments and delays, he sailed on his third voyage, on the 30th of May, 1498. His squadron consisted of six ships only, of no great burden,

burden, and but indifferently provided for so long and dangerous a navigation.

He failed in a different direction to what he had hitherto done, in order to fall in with the coast of India. On the first of August, the man stationed in the round top surprised them with the joyful cry of *land*. They stood towards it, and discovered a considerable island, which the admiral called Trinidad, a name it still retains. He did not arrive at Hispaniola till the 30th of August, when he found the affairs of the colony in such a situation, as afforded him no prospect of enjoying that repose, of which he stood so much in need.

Many revolutions had happened in that country during his absence. His brother, the deputy-governor, in consequence of the advice the admiral gave him before his departure, had removed the colony from Isabella to a more commodious station, on the opposite side of the island, and laid the foundation of St. Domingo. The natives were soon after reduced to the Spanish yoke, which appeared so oppressive to them, that they rose in their own defence, but were easily conquered. At the same time, Roldon, whom Columbus had placed in a station, which required him to be the gardian of order and tranquillity, persuaded the colony to rise in arms.

Such

Such was the diftracted ftate of the colony when Columbus arrived at St. Domingo; but his wifdom and moderation foon brought every thing to order.

While Columbus was thus engaged in the Weft, the fpirit of difcovery did not languifh in Portugal. Emmanuel, who inherited the enterprifing genius of his predeceffors, perfifted in their grand fcheme of opening a paffage to the Eaft Indies by the Cape of Good Hope; and foon after his acceffion to the throne, he equipped a fquadron for that important voyage. He gave the command of it to Vafco de Gama, a man of noble birth, poffeffed of virtue, prudence, and courage, equal to the ftation. The fquadron, like all thofe fitted out for difcovery in the infancy of navigation, was extremely feeble, confifting only of three veffels, of neither burthen nor force adequate to the fervice.

He fet fail from Lifbon on the 9th of July, 1497, and ftanding towards the South, had to ftruggle for four months with contrary winds, before he could reach the Cape of Good Hope: Here their violence began to abate, and during an interval of calm weather, in the latter end of November, Gama doubled that formidable promontory, which had fo long been the boundary of navigation, and directed his courfe towards the north-eaft,

along

along the African coast. He touched at several ports, and after various adventures, he came to an anchor before the city of Meleida. Gama now pursued his voyage with almost absolute certainty of success, and, under the conduct of a Mahometan pilot, he arrived at Calecut, upon the coast of Malabar, on the 22d of May, 1498.

What he beheld of the wealth, the populousness, the cultivation, the industry, and arts of this highly civilized country, far exceeded any idea that he had formed, from the imperfect accounts, which the Europeans had hitherto received of it. But as he possessed neither sufficient force to attempt a settlement, nor proper commodities, with which he could carry on commerce of any consequence, he hastened back to Portugal, with an account of his success in performing a voyage the longest, as well as most difficult, that had ever been made since the first invention of navigation. He landed at Lisbon, on the 14th of September, 1499, two years, two months, and five days from the time he left that port.

Amerigo Vespucci, a Florentine gentleman, having accompanied Ojeda in a voyage to the new world, on his return transmitted an account of his adventures and discoveries to one of his countrymen;

and

and labouring with the vanity of a traveller to magnify his own exploits, he had the addrefs and confidence to frame his narrative, fo as to make it appear, that he had the glory of having firft difcovered the continent in the new world. The country, of which Amerigo was fuppofed to be the difcoverer, came gradually to be called by his name. By the univerfal confent of nations, AMERICA is the name beftowed on this new quarter of the globe. The bold pretenfions of a fortunate impoftor have robbed the difcoverer of the new world of a diftinction which belonged to him. The name of Amerigo has fupplanted that of Columbus, and it is now too late to redrefs the injury.

During the laft year of the fourteenth century, Pedro Alvarez Cabral was fitted out by the king of Portugal, in order to carry on trade, or attempt conquefts, in India, to which place Gama had juft fhewn them the way. In order to avoid the coaft of Africa, where he was certain of meeting with variable breezes, or frequent calms, which might retard his voyage, Cabral ftood out to fea, and kept fo far to the Weft, that, to his furprife, he found himfelf upon the fhore of an unknown country, in the tenth degree beyond the line. The country with which he fell in belongs to that province in South America,

America, now known by the name of Brasil. He landed, and having formed a very high idea of the fertility of the soil, and agreeableness of the climate, he took possession of it for the crown of Portugal, and dispatched a ship to Lisbon with an account of this event, which appeared to be no less important than it was unexpected.

While the Spaniards and Portuguese were daily acquiring more enlarged ideas of the extent and opulence of that quarter of the globe which Columbus had made known to them, he himself, far from enjoying the tranquillity and honours, with which his services should have been recompensed, was struggling with every distress, in which the envy and malevolence of the people under his command, or the ingratitude of the court which he served, could involve him. As soon as the court of Spain began to be prejudiced against Columbus, a fatal resolution was taken. Francis de Bovadilla, a knight of Calatrava, was appointed to repair to Hispaniola, with full powers to enquire into the conduct of Columbus; and, if he should find the charge of maladministration proved, to supercede him, and assume the government of the island. It was impossible to escape, when this preposterous commission made it the interest of the judge to pronounce the person, whom he was sent to try, guilty
of

he urged a claim of juftice or merit with an interefted, ungenerous, and unfeeling prince.

However, Columbus, at laft, prevailed on the court of Spain to fit him out on his fourth expedition, which they were perfuaded to embark in, on the promifed hope of his finding out a fhorter and fafer route to the Eaft Indies. He accordingly failed from Cadiz on the 9th of May, 1502, with only four fmall barks, the largeft of which did not exceed feventy tons in burden. On his arrival at Hifpaniola, he met with the moft ungenerous treatment from the new governor Ovando, who would not fuffer him to enter their harbours.

After various and fruitlefs attempts to difcover a paffage to the Indian ocean, Columbus met with all the difafters to which navigation is expofed. Furious hurricanes, with violent ftorms of thunder and lightning, threatened his deftruction, and at laft drove him on the coaft of Jamica, where his little crazy fleet was wrecked, on the 24th of June, 1503.

The diftrefs of Columbus in this fituation was truly lamentable; but his genius rofe above every thing. He fupported the infolence and cruelty of the inhabitants, the ftill more alarming mutiny of
his

his men, and the infamous conduct of the governor of Hispaniola, till some ships appeared, when the Spaniards quitted an island in which the unfeeling jealousy of Ovando had suffered them to languish above a year.

On the 12th of September, 1504, he set sail for Spain with two ships, and his ill fortune pursued him even in his passage home, being overtaken by a storm, and with the greatest difficulty got back to Spain. On his arrival, he received the fatal news of the death of his patroness Queen Isabella.

Columbus, disgusted with the ingratitude of a monarch, whom he had served with such fidelity and success, exhausted with the fatigues and hardships he had endured, and broken with the infirmities these brought upon him, he ended his life at Valadolid, on the 20th of May, 1506, in the 59th year of his age.

*Memorable Events recorded in this Chapter.*

1492  Columbus sets out on his first voyage.
      Discovers the islands of Cuba and Hispaniola.
1493  Columbus sets out on his second voyage.

1494 Discovers the island of Jamaica.
1498 Third voyage of Columbus.
     He discovers the continent of America.
1499 The Portuguese sail to the East Indies by the way of the Cape of Good Hope.
     On what account the name of AMERICA was given to the New World.
1500 Columbus sent in chains to Spain.
1502 He sets out on his fourth voyage.
     Searches in vain for a passage to the East Indies.
1503 Shipwrecked on the island of Jamaica.
1506 Death of Columbus.

CHAP. III.

## CHAP. III.

THE colony of Hispaniola, before the death of Columbus, had gradually acquired the form of a regular and prosperous state. The humane solicitude of Isabella to protect the Indians from oppression, and particularly the proclamation, by which the Spaniards were prohibited to compel them to work, for some time, it is true, retarded the progress of improvement. The natives, considering every exemption from toil as a supreme felicity, despised every allurement and reward by which they were invited to labour. The Spaniards were not numerous enough, either to work the mines, or cultivate the soil, the distempers peculiar to the climate having carried off great numbers.

In order to save the colony from ruin, Ovando ventured to relax the rigour of some royal edicts that had been sent to him. He made a new distribution of the Indians among the Spaniards, and compelled them to labour for a stated time, in digging the mines, or in cultivating the grounds; but, in order to screen himself from the imputation of having subjected them again to servitude, he enjoined their masters to pay them a certain sum, as the price of their work. But the Indians, after enjoying respite from oppression, though during a short interval, now felt the yoke of bondage to be so galling, that they made several attempts to vindicate their own liberty. However, they were subdued as often as they rose, and the treatment they received from Ovando was both cruel and treacherous.

The attention of the Spaniards was so much engrossed by their operations in the mines of Hispaniola, that the spirit of discovery languished for some time. In 1508, Juan Ponce de Leon, who commanded under Ovando in the eastern district of Hispaniola, passed over to the island of St. Juan de Puerto Rico, which Columbus had discovered in his second voyage, and penetrated into the interior parts of the country. As he found the soil to be fertile, and expected, from some symptons, as well as from the information of the inhabitants, to discover mines of gold in the mountains, Ovando permitted him to attempt making a settlement in the island. In a few years, Puerto Rico was subjected to the Spanish government, the natives were reduced to servitude, and being treated with the same inconsiderate rigour as their neighbours in Hispaniola, the race of original inhabitants, worn

out

worn out with fatigue and sufferings,
was soon exterminated.

Sebastian de Ocampo, by the command
of Ovando, sailed round Cuba, and first
discovered, with certainty, that this
country, which Columbus once supposed
to be a part of the continent, was only
a large island.

This voyage round Cuba was one of the
last occurrences under the administration
of Ovando. Ever since the death of
Columbus, his son Don Diego had been
employed in soliciting Ferdinand to grant
him the offices of Vice-roy and Admiral
in the New World, together with all
the other immunities and profits which
descended to him by inheritance, in consequence of the original capitulation with
his father. But if these dignities and
revenues appeared so considerable to
Ferdinand, that, at the expence of being
deemed unjust, as well as ungrateful, he
had wrested them from Columbus, it is
not surprizing that he should be un-
willing to confer them on his son. Accordingly Don Diego wasted two years in
incessant but fruitless importunity. Weary
of this, he endeavoured at length to obtain, by a legal sentence, what he could
not procure from the favour of an interested monarch. He commenced a suit
against Ferdinand before the council

which

which managed Indian affairs, and that court, with an integrity which reflects honour upon its proceedings, decided against the king, and confirmed all the privileges stipulated in the capitulation. Ferdinand still shewed his repugnance to do Diego justice, nor would he at last have done any thing, had he not been in a manner forced to it by a powerful party, raised in consequence of the marriage of Don Diego with Donna Maria, daughter of Don Ferdinand, great commendator of Leon, and brother of the duke of Alva, a nobleman of the first rank, and nearly related to the king. The duke and his family espoused so warmly the cause of their new ally, that Ferdinand could not resist their solicitations.

In 1509, he recalled Ovando, and appointed Don Diego his successor, though even in conferring this favour, he could not conceal his jealousy; for he allowed him to assume only the title of governor, and not that of vice-roy.

Don Diego immediately set off for Hispaniola, attended by his brother, his uncle, his wife, whom the courtesy of the Spaniards honoured with the title of vice-queen, and a numerous retinue of both sexes, born of good families. He lived with a splendour and magnificence hitherto unknown in the New World, and

the

the family of Columbus seemed now to enjoy the honours and rewards due to his inventive genius, of which he himself had been cruelly defrauded. The colony itself acquired new lustre by the accession of so many inhabitants, of a different rank and character from most of those, who had hitherto emigrated to America, and many of the most illustrious families in the Spanish settlements are descended from the persons, who at that time accompanied Don Diego Columbus.

Juan Diaz de Solis, about this time, set out, in conjunction with Pinzon, upon new discoveries. They sailed due South, towards the equinoctial line, which Pinzon had formerly crossed, and advanced as far as the fortieth degree of southern latitude. They were astonished to find, that the continent of America stretched, on the right hand, through all this vast extent of ocean. They landed in different places, to take possession in the name of their sovereign; but though the country appeared to be extremely fertile and inviting, their force was so small, having been fitted out rather for discovery than making settlements, that they left no colony behind them. Their voyage, however, served to give the Spaniards more exalted and adequate ideas, with respect to the dimensions of the New World.

Private

Private adventurers attempted to make settlements on the new continent; but the loss of their ships by various accidents upon unknown coasts, the diseases peculiar to a climate the most noxious in all America, the want of provisions, unavoidable in a country imperfectly cultivated, dissentions among themselves, and the incessant hostilities of the natives, involved them in a succession of calamities, the bare recital of which would strike my readers with horror.

Notwithstanding the unfortunate issue of this expedition, the Spaniards were not deterred from engaging in new schemes of a similar nature. Juan Ponce de Leon, in 1512. fitted out three ships at his own expence, for a voyage of discovery, and his reputation soon drew together a respectable body of followers. He directed his course towards the Lucayo islands; and, after touching at several of them, as well as of the Bahama isles, he stood to the Southwest, and discovered a country hitherto unknown to the Spaniards, which he called Florida, either because he fell in with it on Palm Sunday, or on account of its gay and beautiful appearance. He attempted to land in different places, but met with such vigorous opposition from the natives, who were fierce and warlike, as convinced him, that an en-

ereafe

crease, of force was requisite to effect a settlement. Satisfied with having opened a communication with a new country, of whose value and importance he conceived very sanguine hopes, he returned to Puerto Rico, through the channel now known by the name of the Gulf of Florida.

Soon after the expedition to Florida, a discovery of much greater importance was made in another part of America. Balboa, having been raised to the government of the small colony at Santa Maria in Darien, made frequent inroads into the adjacent country, and collected a considerable quantity of gold, which abounded more in that part of the continent than in the islands. In one of these excursions, the Spaniards contended with such eagerness about the division of some gold, that they were at the point of proceeding to acts of violence against one another. A young Indian prince, who was present, astonished at the high value they set upon a thing, of which he did not discern the use, tumbled the gold out of the balance with indignation, and, turning to the Spaniards, " Why do you quarrel," (said he) " about such a trifle ? If you are so passionately fond of gold, as to abandon your own country, and to disturb the tranquillity of distant nations for its sake, I will conduct you to a region, where

this

this metal, which seems to be the chief object of your admiration and desire, is so common, that the meanest utensils are formed of it."

Balboa and his companions, transported with what they heard, eagerly enquired where this happy country lay, and how they might arrive at it. He informed them, at the distance of six suns, that is, of six days journey towards the South, they should discover another ocean, near to which this wealty kingdom was situated; but, if they intended to attack that powerful state, they must assemble forces far superior in number and strength to what they were at present. This was the first information which the Spaniards received concerning the southern ocean, or the opulent and extensive country, known afterwards by the name of Peru.

Balboa, having mustered all the forces he could, which amounted only to 190 men, set out on this important expedition on the first of September, 1513, about the time that the periodical rains began to abate. Though their guides had represented the breath of the isthmus to be only a journey of six days, they had already spent twenty-five in forcing their way through the woods and mountains. Many of them were ready to sink under such uninterrupted fatigue in that sultry climate,

climate, several were seized with the diseases peculiar to the country, and all became impatient to reach the period of their labours and sufferings. At length, the Indians assured them, that from the top of the next mountain they should discover the ocean which was the object of their wishes. When, with infinite toil, they had climbed up the greater part of that steep ascent, Balboa commanded his men to halt, and advanced alone to the summit, that he might be the first who should enjoy such a spectacle which he had so long desired. As soon as he beheld the South Sea stretching in endless prospect below him, he fell on his knees, and lifting up his hands to heaven, returned thanks to God, who had conducted him to a discovery so beneficial to his country, and so honourable to himself. His followers, observing his transports of joy, rushed forward to join his wonder, exultation, and gratitude. They held on their course to the shore, with great alacrity, when Balboa advancing up to the middle in the waves, with his buckler and sword, took possession of that ocean in the name of the king his master, and vowed to defend it.

That part of the great Pacific or Southern ocean, which Balboa first discovered, still retains the name of the Gulf of St. Michael, which he gave to it, and is situated

ated to the east of Panama. From several of the petty princes, who governed in the districts adjacent to that gulf, he extorted provisions and gold by force of arms; others sent them to him voluntarily. Together with the acquisition of this wealth, which served to soothe and encourage his followers, he received accounts which confirmed his sanguine hopes of future and more extensive benefits from this expedition. All the people on the coast of the South Sea concurred in informing him, that there was a mighty and opulent kingdom situated at a considerable distance towards the south-east, where gold was found in plenty.

Though the information Balboa received from the people, on the coast, as well as his own conjectures and hopes, made him extremely impatient to visit this unknown country, his prudence restrained him from attempting to invade it with a handful of men, exhausted by fatigue, and weakened by diseases. He determined to lead back his followers to their settlement at Santa Maria in Darien, and to return next season with a force more adequate to such an arduous enterprize. He reached Santa Maria after an absence of four months, with greater glory and more treasure, than the Spaniards ever had acquired in any former expedition in the New World.

He

He took care to acquaint the court of Spain with the important difcovery he had made, and demanded a reinforcement of a thoufand men, in order to attempt the conqueft of that opulent country, concerning which he had received fuch inviting intelligence.

The meanneffes and jealoufies of Ferdinand, and the advice of men around him worfe than himfelf, induced him to fupercede Balboa, the moft proper man he could have employed, and to appoint Pedrarias Davila governor of Darien. He gave him the command of fourteen ftout veffels, and twelve hundred foldiers. Thefe were fitted out at the public expence, and granted with a liberality unufual to Ferdinand.

Perdrarias reached the gulf of Darien without any remarkable accident, in July, 1514; but his ill conduct, and bafe treatment of Balboa, ftopped all operations, and nearly ruined this flourifhing colony. Both parties fent home complaints to Spain againft each other.

At length, Ferdinand became fenfible of his imprudence in fuperceding the moft active and experienced officer he had in the New World, and, by way of compenfation to Balboa, he appointed him lieutenant-governor of the countries upon the South Sea, with very extenfive privileges and authority,

authority, at the same time ordering Pedrarias to support him in all his operations, and to consult him on every measure which he himself pursued. Surely nothing could be more ridiculous and absurd in Ferdinand than this conduct! Padrarias now conceived the most implacable hatred to Balboa, and, though he afterwards seemed so far reconciled to him, as to give him his daughter in marriage, he soon found means falsely to accuse him of high treason, had him tried, condemned, and publicly executed, in 1517. Pedrarias, notwithstanding the violence and injustice of his proceedings, was not only screened from punishment by the powerful patronage of the infamous bishop of Burgos, an inveterate enemy to real merit, but continued in the government.

While matters were thus going forward in Darien, several important events occurred with respect to the discovery, the conquest, and government of other provinces in the New World. Ferdinand was so intent upon opening a communication with the Molucca or Spice Islands by the west, that, in the year 1515, he fitted out two ships at his own expence, in order to attempt such a voyage, and gave the command of them to Juan Diaz de Solis, who was deemed one of the most skilful navigators in Spain. He stood along the coast of
South

The Beheading of Balloon.

South America, and on the first of January, 1516, he entered a river which he called Janeiro, where an extensive commerce is now carried on. From thence he proceeded to a spacious bay, which he supposed to be the entrance into a strait that communicated with the Indian ocean; but, upon advancing farther, he found it to be the mouth of Rio de Plata, one of the vast rivers, by which the southern continent of America is watered. In endeavouring to make a descent in this country, De Solis and several of his crew were slain by the natives; who, in sight of the ships, cut their bodies in pieces, roasted and devoured them. Discouraged by the loss of their commander, and terrified at this shocking spectacle, the surviving Spaniards set sail for Europe, without aiming at any further discovery. Though this attempt proved abortive, it was not without benefit: it turned the attention of ingenious men to this course of navigation, and prepared the way for a more fortunate voyage.

While discoveries were thus going forward, Hispaniola continued as their principal colony, and the seat of government. Don Diego Columbus wanted neither inclination nor abilities to have rendered the members of this colony, who were most immediately under his direction, prosperous and happy; but he was circumscribed in all his operations by the suspicious policy of Ferdinand, who on every occasion, and under the most frivolous pretexts, retrenched his privileges, and encouraged the treasurer, the judges, and other subordinate officers, to counteract his measures, and to dispute his authority. In short, Ferdinand's conduct was so ungenerous, as obliged Don Diego to quit Hispaniola, and repair to Spain, in order to seek redress for his injuries.

On the death of Ferdinand, in 1517, Charles V. took possession of the government. Diego Velasquez, who conquered Cuba in the year 1511, still retained the government of that island, as the deputy of Don Diego Columbus, though he seldom acknowledged his superior, and aimed at rendering his own authority altogether independant. Under his prudent administration, Cuba became one of the most flourishing of the Spanish settlements. The fame of this drew many persons from the other colonies, expecting there to find some permanent establishment, or some employment for their activity. As Cuba lay to the west of all the islands possessed by the Spaniards, and as the ocean which stretches beyond it towards that quarter, had not hitherto been explored, these circumstances naturally invited the inhabitants to attempt new discoveries.

An

An expedition for this purpose, in which activity and resolution might conduct to sudden wealth, was more suited to the genius of the age, than the patient industry requisite in clearing ground, and manufacturing sugar. Hence it happened, that several officers who had served under Pedrarias in Darien, entered into an association to undertake a voyage of discovery. They persuaded Francisco Hernandez Cordova, an opulent planter in Cuba, and a man of great courage, to join with them in the adventure, and chose him to be their commander. Velasquez not only approved of the design, but assisted in carrying it on.

Three smalls vessels were purchased, and furnished with every thing requisite either for traffic or war. An hundred and ten men embarked on board them, and sailed from St. Jago de Cuba on the 8th of February, 1517.

On the twenty-first day after their departure from St. Jago, they saw land, which proved to be Cape Catoche, the eastern point of that large peninsula projecting from the continent of America, which still retains its original name of Yucatan. As they approached the shore, five canoes came off full of people decently clad in cotton garments: an astonishing sight to the Spaniards, who had found every other part of America possessed by native savages. Cordova endeavoured by small presents to gain the good-will of these people. They, though amazed at the strange objects now presented for the first time to their view, invited the Spaniards to visit their habitations, with an appearance of cordiality. They landed accordingly, and as they advanced into the country, they observed with new wonder some large houses built with stone; but they soon found, if the Yucatans had made progress in improvement beyond their countrymen, they were likewise more artful and warlike. Though the Indian chief received Cordova with many tokens of friendship, he had posted a considerable body of his subjects in ambush behind a thicket, who, upon a signal given by him, rushed out and attacked the Spaniards with great boldness, and with some degree of martial order. At the first flight of their arrows, fifteen of the Spaniards were wounded; but the Indians were so terrified with the sudden explosion of the fire-arms, and so surprised at the execution done by them, by the cross-bows, and by the other weapons of their new enemies, that they precipitately fled. Cordova immediately quitted a country where he had met with so unwelcome a reception, carrying off

off two prisoners, with the ornaments of a small temple which he plundered in making his retreat to his ship.

Cordova continued his course towards the west without losing sight of the coast, and on the sixteenth day arrived at Campeachy. At this place the natives received them more kindly; but the Spaniards were much surprised, that on all the extensive coast along which they had sailed, they had not met with any river. Their water beginning to fail, they advanced in hopes of finding a supply; and at length they discovered the mouth of a river.

Cordova landed all his troops in order to protect the sailors, whose business it was to fill the casks; but the natives rushed down upon them with such fury, and in such numbers, that forty-seven of the Spaniards were killed upon the spot, and one man only of the whole body escaped unhurt. Their commander, though wounded in twelve different places, directed the retreat with presence of mind equal to the courage with which he had led them on in the engagement, and with much difficulty they reached their ships. Having met with this terrible repulse, nothing remained but to hasten back to Cuba with their shattered forces. In their passage thither, they suffered the greatest distress from the want of water,

that

that men wounded and fickly, fhut up in
fmall veffels, and expofed to the heat of
the torrid zone, can be fuppofed to fuffer. Some died on their paffage, and
Cordova their commander, foon after he
landed at Cuba, paid the debt of nature.

Unfortunate as this expedition proved,
it contributed rather to animate than
damp a fpirit of enterprize among the
Spaniards. They had difcovered an extenfive country, fituated in the neighbourhood of Cuba, fertile in appearance,
and poffeffed by a people far more refined
than any they had hitherto met with in
America. Velafquez, through particular
views of ambition and intereft, not only
encouraged their ardour, but at his own
expence fitted out four fhips for the voyage.
Two hundred and forty volunteers, among
whom were feveral perfons of rank and
fortune, embarked in this enterprife. The
command of it was given to Juan de
Grijalva, a young man of known merit
and courage, with inftructions attentively
to obferve the nature of the countries
which he fhould difcover; to barter for
gold; and, if circumftances were inviting,
to fettle a colony in fome proper ftation.
He failed from St. Jago de Cuba, on the
8th. of April, 1518.

They held the fame courfe as in the
former voyage, and at laft reached Potonchan,

tonchan, where the laſt adventurers had been ſo roughly handled. The deſire of avenging their countrymen who had been ſlain there, concurred with their ideas of good policy, in prompting them to land, that they might chaſtize the Indians with ſuch exemplary rigour, as would ſtrike terror into all the people around them; but, though they diſimbarked all their troops, and carried aſhore ſome field pieces, the Indians fought with ſuch courage, that the Spaniards with difficulty gained the victory; and were confirmed in their opinion, that the inhabitants of this country would prove more formidable enemies than any they had met with in other parts of America.

From Potonchan, they continued their voyage towards the weſt, keeping as near as poſſible to the ſhore, and caſting anchor every evening, from dread of the dangerous accidents to which they might be expoſed in an unknown ſea. During the day their eyes were turned continually towards land, with a mixture of ſurprize and wonder at the beauty of the country, as well as the novelty of the objects they beheld. Many villages were ſcattered along the coaſt, in which they could diſtinguiſh houſes of ſtone that appeared white and lofty at a diſtance. One of the ſoldiers happening to remark, that this country
resembled

resembled Spain in its appearance, Grijalva, with universal applause, called it New Spain, the name which still distinguishes this extensive and opulent province of the Spanish empire in America.

On the 9th of June, they landed in a river, which the natives called Tabasco, and the fame of their victory at Potonchan having reached this place, the chief not only received them amicably, but bestowed presents upon them of such value, as confirmed the high ideas, which the Spaniards had formed with respect to the wealth and fertility of the country. These ideas were raised still higher, by what occurred at the place where they next touched. This was considerably to the west of Tabasco, in the province since known by the name of Guaxaca. There they were received with the respect due to superior beings. The people perfumed them as they landed with gum copal, and presented to them as offerings the choicest delicacies of their country. They were extremely fond of trading with their new visitants, and in six days the Spaniards obtained ornaments of gold, of curious workmanship, to the value of fifteen thousand pesos, in exchange for European toys of small price. The two prisoners, whom Cordova had brought from Yucatan, had hitherto served as interpreters; but as they were unacquainted with

with the language of this country, the
Spaniards learned from the natives by
signs, that they were the subjects of a
great monarch, called Montezuma, whose
dominions extended over that and many
other provinces.

Leaving this province, with which he
had so much reason to be contented, Grijalva continued his course towards the west.
He landed on a small island, which he named the Isle of Sacrifices, because there the
Spaniards beheld the horrid spectacle of human victims, which the barbarous superstitions of the natives offered to their gods.
He touched at another small island, which
he called St. Juan de Ulua.

From this place he dispatched Pedro de
Alvarado, one of his officers, to Velasquez,
with a full account of the important discoveries he had made, and with all the
treasure that he had acquired by trafficking
with the natives. After the departure of
Alvarado, he himself, with the remaining
vessels, proceeded along the coast as far
as the river Panuco, the country still appearing to be well peopled, fertile, and
opulent.

It was the opinion of several of Grijalva's officers, that it was not enough to
have discovered those delightful regions,
or to have performed, at their different
landing-places, the empty ceremony of
taking

taking poffeffion of them for the crown of Caftile, and that their glory was incomplete, unlefs they planted a colony in fome proper ftation, which might not only fecure the Spanifh nation a footing in the country; but, with the reinforcements they were certain of receiving, might gradually fubject the whole to the dominion of their fovereign. However, the fquadron had now been above five months at fea, the greater part of their provifions were exhaufted, and what remained of their ftores fo much corrupted by the heat of the climate, as to be almoft unfit for ufe; they had loft fome men by death, and others were fickly; the country was crouded with people, who feemed to be intelligent as well as brave, and they were under the government of one powerful monarch, who could bring them to act againft their invaders with united force. To plant a colony under fo many correfponding difficulties, appeared a matter too hazardous to be attempted. Though Grijalva was not without ambition and courage, yet he was deftitute of the fuperior abilities requifite to form and execute fo extenfive a plan. He judged it more prudent to return to Cuba, having fulfilled the purpofe of his voyage, and accomplifhed every thing, which the armament he commanded enabled him to perform. He returned to St. Jago de Cuba,

Cuba, on the 26th of October, from whence he had failed about six months, without having met with any material accident.

As this was the longest, so it had been the most successful voyage the Spaniards had hitherto made in the New World. They had discovered that Yucatan was not an island, as they had supposed, but part of the great continent of America. From Potonchan they had pursued their course for many hundred miles along a coast formerly unexplored, stretching at first towards the west, and then turning to the north. All the country they discovered appeared to be no less valuable than extensive. As soon as Avarado reached Cuba, Velasquez, transported with success so far beyond his most sanguine expectations, immediately dispatched a person of confidence to carry this important intelligence to Spain; to exhibit the rich productions of the countries which had been discovered by his means; and to solicit such an increase of authority, as might enable and encourage him to attempt the conquest of them. Without waiting for the return of his messenger, or for the arrival of Grijalva, of whom he was become so jealous or distrustful that he resolved no longer to employ him, he began to prepare such a powerful armament, as might

H prove

prove equal to an enterprise of so much danger and importance. The little and mean jealousies, which the Spaniards seem naturally to entertain of every man of merit, is a very singular blemish in the character of that nation.

The expedition, for which Velasquez was now preparing with so much ardour and activity, had in its views conquests far beyond what the Spanish nation had hitherto accomplished. It led them to the knowledge of a people, who, if compared with those tribes of South America, and the West Indies, with whom they were hitherto acquainted, were infinitely more civilized, and far better acquainted with the arts of war, and the sciences in general. Before we proceed to the history of events extremely different from those we have already related, it may not be improper to take a view of the state of the New World, such as it was when first discovered, and to contemplate the policies and manners of the rude uncultived tribes, by whom the different parts of it were occupied, and with whom the Spaniards at this time had intercourse. This shall be the subject of our next chapter.

*Memorable*

*Memorable Events recorded in this Chapter.*

1505   War with the American Indians.
1508   New discoveries and settlements.
       Diego Columbus appointed governor of Hispaniola.
1510   Cuba conquered.
1512   Florida discovered.
1513   The South Sea discovered.
       Pedrarias appointed governor of Darien.
1517   Balboa executed by the order of the treacherous Pedrarias.
       Death of Ferdinand, king of Spain; succeeded by Charles V.
       Yucatan discovered.
1518   Campeachy discovered.
       Grijalva discovers New Spain, Tobasco, Guaxaca, and St. Juan de Ulua.

## CHAP. IV.

THE immense extent of the New World is a circumstance that strikes us with wonder. America is remarkable, not only for its magnitude, but for its position. It stretches from the northern polar circle to a high southern latitude, above fifteen hundred miles beyond the farthest extremity of the old continent on that side of the line. Next to its extent, the grandeur of the objects which it presents to our view is most apt to strike the eye of an observer. Nature seems to have carried on her operations upon a larger scale, with a bolder hand, and to have distinguished the features of this country by a peculiar magnificence. The mountains of America are much superior in height to those in the other divisions of the globe. Even the plain of Quito, which may be considered as the base of the Andes, is elevated farther above the sea, than the top of the Pyrenees. From those lofty mountains descend rivers proportionably large, with which the streams in the ancient continent are not to be compared, either for length or course, or the vast body of water, which they roll towards the ocean. Their lakes are no less

less conspicuous for grandeur than their mountains and rivers. They may properly be termed inland seas of fresh water.

The temperature of the climate of America, and the different laws to which it is subject with respect to the distribution of heat and cold, are marks which particularly distinguish it from other parts of the earth. Throughout all these vast regions, there were only two monarchies remarkable for extent of territory, or distinguished by any progress in improvement. The rest of their continent was possessed by small independent tribes, destitute of arts and industry, and neither capable to correct the defects, nor desirous to meliorate the condition of that part of the earth allotted to them for their habitation. Countries, occupied by such people, were almost in the same state as if they had been without inhabitants.

Notwithstanding the vast extent of America, and the variety of its climates, the different species of animals peculiar to it are much fewer in proportion, than those of the other hemisphere. In the islands, there are only four kinds of quadrupeds known, the largest of which did not exceed the size of a rabbit. On the continent, the variety was greater; and though the individuals of each kind could not fail of multiplying exceedingly, when almoſt unmoleſted by men, who were neither ſo numerous, nor ſo united in ſociety, as to be formidable enemies to the animal creation, yet the number of diſtinct ſpecies muſt be conſidered as extremely ſmall.

To the cauſes, **which** checked the growth and vigour of the more noble animals, may be attributed the propagation and encreaſe **of** reptiles and inſects. The air is often darkened with clouds of inſects, and **the** ground covered with ſhocking and noxious reptiles.

The American birds of the torrid zone, like thoſe of the ſame climate in Aſia and Africa, are decked in plumage, which dazzles the eye with the beauty of its colours; but nature, ſatisfied with clothing them in this gay dreſs, has denied moſt of them that melody of ſound, and variety of **notes, which** catch and delight the ear. Let **my youthful** readers ſtop here, and pauſe for a while; through all the conditions and circumſtances of life, they will find, on reflection, that the hand of Providence has diſtributed things more equally than they are aware of, as well in the human, as in the feathered race.

In a continent ſo extenſive as America, the nature of the ſoil muſt be various.

In

In each of its provinces, we find some distinguishing peculiarity, the description of which belongs to those who write their particular history, and would be an idle attempt to describe in this epitome.

How America was first peopled, by what course mankind migrated from one continent to the other, and in what quarter it is most probable the communication was first opened between them, are matters for which we have little grounds to go upon beyond that of conjecture. The theories and speculations of ingenious men, with respect to this subject, would fill many volumes; but they are often so wild and chimerical, that it would be offering an insult to the understanding of our readers, to attempt either to enumerate or refute them, even provided the limits of this work would admit of it.

To enquire into the character and condition of the American nations, at the time when they became known to the Europeans, deserves more attentive consideration, than the enquiry concerning their original. The discovery of the New World enlarged the sphere of contemplation, and presented nations to our view in a state very rude and uncultivated. The greater part of its inhabitants were strangers to industry and labour, ignorant of arts, imperfectly acquainted with the

nature

nature of property, and enjoying almost without restriction or controul the blessings which flowed spontaneously from the bounty of nature. Among the small independent tribes of South America, their customs, manners, and institutions, were nearly similar, and so extremely rude, that the denomination of *savages* may be applied to them all. The Spaniards, who first visited America, and who had opportunity of beholding its various tribes, while entire and unsubdued, were far from possessing the qualities requisite for observing the striking spectacle presented to their view. Neither the age in which they lived, nor the nation to which they belonged, had made such progress in true science as inspires enlarged and liberal sentiments. The conquerors of the New World were mostly illiterate adventurers, destitute of all the ideas which should have directed them in contemplating objects, so extremely different from those with which they were acquainted. Surrounded continually with danger, or struggling with hardships, they had little leisure, and less capacity, for any speculative enquiry. Eager to take possession of a country of such extent and opulence, and happy in finding it occupied by inhabitants so incapable to defend it, they hastily pronounced them to be a wretched order of men, formed merely for servitude; and were more employed in computing the profits of their labour, than in enquiring into the operations of their minds, or the reason of their customs and institutions.

The human body is less affected by climate than that of any other animal. Some animals are confined to a particular region of the globe, and cannot exist beyond it; while others, though they may be brought to bear the injuries of a foreign climate, cease to multiply when carried from their native air and soil. Even such as seem capable of being naturalized in various climates, feel the effect of every remove from their proper station, and gradually dwindle and degenerate from the vigour and perfection peculiar to their species. Man is the only living creature, whose frame is at once so hardy and so flexible, that he can spread over the whole earth, become the inhabitant of every region, and thrive and multiply under every climate, though not without some attending inconveniences.

The complexion of the Americans is of a reddish brown, nearly resembling the colour of copper. Their persons are of a full size, extremely strait, and well proportioned; but they are more remarkable for agility than strength. As the external form of the

Americans

Americans leads us to suspect, that there is some natural debility in their frame, the smallness of their appetite for food has been mentioned by many authors as a confirmation of this suspicion. The quantity of food which men consume varies according to the temperature of the climate in which they live, the degree of activity which they exert, and the natural vigour of their constitutions. Under the enervating heat of the torrid zone, and where men pass their days in indolence and ease, they require less nourishment than the active inhabitants of temperate or cold countries.

Notwithstanding the feeble make of the Americans, hardly any of them are deformed, mutilated, or defective in any of their senses. All travellers have been struck with this circumstance, and have celebrated the uniform symmetry and perfection of their external figure.

In the simplicity of the savage state, when man is not oppressed with labour, or enervated by luxury, or disquieted with care, we are apt to imagine, that his life will flow on almost untroubled by disease or suffering, until his days be terminated, in extreme old age, by the gradual decays of nature. We find, accordingly, among the Americans, as well as among other rude people, persons,
whose

whose decrepid and shrivilled forms seem to indicate an extraordinary length of life; but as most of them are unacquainted with the art of numbering, and all of them as forgetful of what is past, as they are improvident for what is to come, it is impossible to ascertain their age with any degree of precision.

Whatever may be the situation in which man is placed, he is born to suffer; and his diseases, in the savage state, though fewer in number, are, like those of the animals, whom he nearly resembles in his mode of life, more violent and more fatal. If luxury engenders and nourishes distempers of one species, the rigour and distress of savage life bring on those of another. As men, in this state, are wonderfully improvident, and their means of subsistence precarious, they often pass from extreme want to exuberant plenty, according to the vicissitudes of fortune in the chase, or in consequence of the various degree of abundance, with which the earth affords to them its productions in different seasons. Their inconsiderate gluttony in the one situation, and their severe abstinence in the other, are equally pernicious. The strength and vigour of savages are at some seasons, impaired by what they suffer from scarcity of food; at others,
they

they are afflicted with disorders arising
from indigestion and a superfluity of gross
aliment. These are so common, that
they may be considered as the unavoidable
consequence of their mode of subsisting,
and cut off considerable numbers in the
prime of life. There are other disorders,
to which they are continually exposed,
owing to the inclemency of different
seasons. In the savage state, hardships
and fatigues violently assault the constitution;
in polished societies, intemperance
undermines it. It is not easy
to determine, which of them operates
with most fatal effects, or tends most to
abridge human life.

The thoughts and attention of a savage
are confined within the small circle of
objects, immediately conducive to his
preservation or enjoyment. Every thing
beyond that is beneath his observations,
or is entirely indifferent to him. Like
a mere animal, what is before his eyes
interests and affects him; what is out of
sight, or at a distance, makes little impression.
They follow blindly the impulse
of the appetite they feel, but are entirely
regardless of distant consequences, and
even of those removed in the least degree
from immediate apprehension.

The active efforts of their minds are
few and languid. The desires of simple
                                        nature

nature are very limited, and where a favourable climate yields almoſt ſpontaneouſly what ſuffices to gratify them, they ſcarcely ſtir the ſoul, or excite any violent emotion. Hence the people of ſeveral tribes in America waſte their lives in a ſtate of indolence.

To be free from occupation, ſeems to be all the enjoyment to which they aſpire. Such is their averſion to labour, that neither the hope of future good, nor the apprehenſion of evil, can ſurmount it. They appear equally indifferent to both, diſcovering little ſolicitude, and taking no precaution to avoid the one, or to ſecure the other. The cravings of hunger may rouſe them; but as they devour, with little diſtinction, whatever will appeaſe its inſtinctive demands, the exertions theſe occaſion are of ſhort duration.

Amongſt the rudeſt tribes in America, a regular union between huſband and wife was univerſal, and the rights of marriage were underſtood and recognized. In thoſe diſtricts where ſubſiſtence was ſcanty, and the difficulty of maintaining a family was great, the man confined himſelf to one wife. In warmer and more fertile provinces, the facility of procuring food concurred with the influence of climate, in inducing the inhabitants to encreaſe the number of their wives. In ſome countries,

tries, the marriage union subsisted during life; in others, the impatience of the Americans under restraint of any species, together with their natural levity and caprice, prompted them to dissolve it on very slight pretexts, and often without assigning any cause.

' The situation of the American women, in whatever light we consider them, was equally humiliating and miserable. Among many people of America, the marriage contract is properly a purchase. The man buys his wife of her parents. Though unacquainted with the use of money, or with such commercial transactions as take place in more improved society, he knows how to give an equivalent for an object he desires to possess. In some places, the suitor devotes his service for a certain time to the parent of the maid whom he courts; in others, he hunts for them occasionally, or assists in cultivating their fields, and forming their canoes; in others, he offers presents of such things as are deemed most valuable on account of their usefulness or rarity. In return for these, he receives his wife; and this circumstance, added to the low estimation of women among savages, leads him to consider her as a female servant whom he has purchased, and whom he has a title to treat as an inferior. The condition

dition of an American woman is so peculiarly grievous, and their depression so complete, that servitude is a name too mild to describe their wretched state. A wife, among most tribes, is no better than a beast of burden, destined to every office of labour and fatigue. While the men loiter out the day in sloth, or spend it in amusement, the women are condemned to incessant toil. Tasks are imposed upon them without pity, and services are received without complacence or gratitude. Every circumstance reminds women of this mortifying inferiority. They must approach their lords with reverence, regard them as more exalted beings, and are not permitted to eat in their presence.

The Americans are not deficient in affection and attachment to their offspring. They feel the power of this instinct in its full force, and as long as their progeny continue feeble and helpless, no people exceed them in tenderness and care. In the simplicity of the savage state, the affections of parents, like the instinctive fondness of animals, ceases almost entirely as soon as their offspring attain maturity. Little instruction fits them for that mode of life to which they are destined. The parents, as if their duty were accomplished, when they have conducted their children through the helpless years of infancy, leave them afterwards at entire liberty. In an American hut, a father, a mother, and their posterity, live together like persons assembled by accident, without seeming to feel the obligation of the duties mutually arising from such connection.

Though the people of America may be all comprehended under the general denomination of savage, the advances they had made in the art of procuring to themselves a certain and plentiful subsistence, were very unequal. On the vast plains of South America, man appears in one of the rudest states, in which he possibly can exist, several tribes depending entirely upon the bounty of nature for subsistence. They discover no solicitude, they employ little foresight, and scarcely exert any industry, to secure what is necessary for their support. The roots which the earth produces spontaneously, the fruits, the berries, and the seeds, which they gather in the woods, together with lizards and other reptiles, which multiply amazingly with the heat of the climate in a fat soil, moistened by frequent rains, supply them with food during some part of the year. At other times they live upon fish; and nature seems to have indulged the laziness of the South American tribes by her liberalities in this way. The vast rivers

of

of that part of America abound with an infinite variety of delicate fish, and are so numerous as to be caught with little trouble. None but tribes contiguous to great rivers can support themselves in this manner. The greater part of the American nations, dispersed over the forests with which their country is covered, do not procure subsistence with the same facility; but are obliged to obtain it by hunting, which in many parts is their principal occupation, and which requires strenuous exertions.

As game and fish are the principal food of the Americans, their agriculture is neither extensive nor laborious. Their principal productions in this line are maze, manioc, plantain, potatoes, and pimento. All the fruits of their industry, together with what their soil and climate produced spontaneously, afforded them but a scanty maintenance. Though their demands for food were very sparing, they hardly raised what was sufficient for their own consumption.

In America, the word nation is not of the same import as in other parts of the globe. It is applied to small societies, perhaps not exceeding two or three hundred persons, but occupying provinces larger than some kingdoms in Europe. In the provinces which border on the Oronoco,

Oronoco, one may travel several hundred miles, in different directions, without finding a single hut, or observing the footsteps of a human creature.

The Americans had no idea of property. As the animals on which the hunter feeds are not bred under his inspection, nor nourished by his care, he can claim no right to them while they run wild in the forest. The forests, or hunting grounds, are deemed the property of the tribe, from which it has a title to exclude every rival nation; but no individual arrogates a right to any district of these, in preference to his fellow-citizen.

We shall now proceed to take a cursory view of their art of war. Savage nations, in carrying on their public wars, are influenced by the same ideas, and animated with the same spirit, as in prosecuting private vengeance. The maxims by which they regulate their military operations, though extremely different from those, which take place among more civilized and populous nations, are well suited to their own political state, and the nature of the country in which they act. They never take the field in numerous bodies, as it would require a greater effort of foresight and industry, than is usual among savages, to provide for their subsistence, during a march of some hundred miles through

through dreary forests, or during a long voyage upon their lakes and rivers.

Their armies are not encumbered with baggage or military stores. Each warrior, besides his arms, carries a mat and a small bag of pounded maize, and with these he is completely equipped for any service. While at a distance from the enemies frontier, they disperse through the woods, and support themselves with the game they kill, and the fish they catch. The manner in which they attack their enemies, the treatment of their prisoners, and the surprizing fortitude they shew in bearing the most cruel tortures, being nearly the same among the South American Indians as among those of the North, we shall not here repeat what we have already mentioned on that head in our History of North America.

In the warmer and more mild climates of America, none of the rude tribes were cloathed. To most of them Nature had not even suggested any Idea of impropriety of being altogether uncovered. As under a mild climate there was little need of any defence from the injuries of the air, and their extreme indolence shunned every species of labour to which it was not urged by absolute necessity, all the inhabitants of the isles, and a considerable part of the people on the continent, remained in this
state

state of naked simplicity. Others were satisfied with some slight covering, such as decency required; but though naked, they were not unadorned. They fastened bits of gold or shells, or shining stones, in their ears, their noses, and cheeks. They stained their skins with a great variety of figures, and they spent much time, and submitted to great pain, in ornamenting their persons in this fantastic manner.

In one part of their dress, which, at first sight appears the most singular and capricious, the Americans have discovered considerable sagacity in providing against the chief inconveniences of their climate, which is often sultry, and moist to excess. All the different tribes, which remain unclothed, are acustomed to anoint and rub their bodies with the grease of animals, with viscous gums, and with oils of different kinds. By this they check that profuse perspiration, which in the torrid zone, wastes the vigour of the frame, and abridges the period of human life. By this too they provide a defence against the extreme moisture during the rainy season. They likewise, at certain seasons, temper paint of different colours with those unctious substances, and bedaub themselves plentifully with that composition. Sheathed with this impenetrable varnish,

their

their skins are not only protected from the penetrating heat of the sun, but, as all the innumerable tribes of insects have an antipathy to the smell or taste of that mixture, they are delivered from their teazing persecutions, which amidst forests and marshes, especially in the warmer regions, would have been wholly insupportable in a state of perfect nakedness.

Savage nations, being far from that state of improvement, in which the mode of living is considered as a mark of distinction, and unacquainted with those wants, which require a variety of accommodations, regulate the construction of their houses according to their limited ideas of necessity. Some of the American tribes were so extremely rude, and had advanced so little beyond the primeval simplicity of nature, that they had no houses at all. During the day, they took shelter from the scorching rays of the sun under thick trees, and at night they formed a shed with their branches and leaves. In the rainy seasons, they retired into caves, formed by the hand of nature, or hollowed out by their own industry. Others, who had no fixed abode, and roamed through the forest in quest of game, sojourned in temporary huts, which they erected with little labour, and abandoned without any concern.

Clubs

Clubs made of some heavy wood, stakes hardened in the fire, lances whose heads were armed with flint or the bone of some animal, are weapons known to the rudest nations. All these, however, were of use only in close encounter; but men wished to annoy their enemies while at a distance, and the bow and arrow is the most early invention for this purpose. The people in some provinces of Chili, and those of Patagonia, towards the southern extremity of America, use a weapon peculiar to themselves. They fasten stones, about the size of a man's fist, to each end of a leather thong of eight feet in length, and swinging these round their heads, throw them with such dexterity, that they seldom miss the object they aim at.

As their food and habitations are perfectly simple, their domestic utensils are few and rude. Some of the southern tribes discovered the art of forming vessels of earthen ware, and baking them in the sun, so as they could endure the fire. These vessels they used in preparing part of their provisions, and this may be considered as a step towards refinement and luxury; for men in their rudest state were not acquainted with any method of dressing their victuals, but by roasting them on the fire, and among several tribes
in

in America this is the only species of cookery yet known.

What appears to be the master-piece of art among the savages of America is the construction of their canoes. An Indian, shut up in his boat of whalebone, covered with skins, can brave that stormy ocean, on which he is compelled to depend for part of his subsistence. The inhabitants of the isles in South America form their canoes by hollowing the trunk of a large tree, with infinite labour, and though in appearance they are extremely aukward and unwieldly, they paddle and steer them with such dexterity, that Europeans, well acquainted with all the improvements in the science of navigation, have been astonished at the rapidity of their motion, and the quickness of their evolutions.

With respect to their religion, even among those tribes, whose religious system was more enlarged, and who had formed some conception of benevolent beings, which delighted in conferring benefits, as well as of malicious powers prone to inflict evil, superstition still appears as the offspring of fear, and all its efforts were employed to avert calamities. They were persuaded that their good deities, prompted by the beneficence of their nature, would bestow every blessing in their power, without solicitation or acknowledgement; and their

their only anxiety was to footh and deprecate the wrath of the powers, whom they regarded as the enemies of mankind.

With respect to the immortality of the foul, the fentiments of the Americans were more united. The human mind, even when leaft improved and invigorated by culture, fhrinks from the thoughts of diffolution, and looks forward with hope and expectation to a ftate of future exiftence. The moft uncivilized favages of America do not apprehend death as the extinction of being: all entertain hopes of a future and more happy ftate, where they fhall be for ever exempt from the calamities, which embitter human life in its prefent condition. This future ftate they conceive to be a delightful country, bleffed with perpetual fpring, whofe forefts abound with game, whofe rivers fwarm with fifh, where famine is never felt, and uninterrupted plenty fhall be enjoyed without labour or toil.

As the difeafes of men in the favage ftate are like thofe of the animal creation, few but extremely violent, their impatience under what they fuffer, and folicitude for the recovery of health, foon infpired them with extraordinary reverence for fuch as pretended to underftand the nature of their maladies, or to preferve them from their fudden and fatal effects. However, thefe
ignorant

ignorant pretenders being such utter strangers to the structure of the human frame, as to know neither the causes of disorders, nor the manner in which they were likely to terminate, superstition, frequently mingled with some portion of craft, supplied what they wanted in knowledge. They imputed the origin of diseases to supernatural influence, and advised or performed a variety of superstitious rites, which they represented to be sufficient to remove the most obstinate and dangerous disorders.

From the superstition and credulity of the Americans likewise proceeded their faith in dreams, their observation of omens, their attention to the chirping of birds, and the cries of animals, all which they supposed to be indications of future events; and if any one of their prognostics was deemed unfavourable, they eagerly abandoned the object they had in pursuit.

Savage as the Americans were, they were not without their amusements; and of these dancing appears to be the principal. The war-dance seems to be the most striking, in which are represented all the manœuvres of an American campaign. Their songs and dances are mostly solemn and martial, they are connected with some of the most serious and important affairs of life, and, having no relation to love,

K                                                          or or gallantry, are seldom common to the two sexes, but executed by the men and women apart.

The Americans are universally fond of gaming. Though they are at other times so indifferent, phlegmatic, silent, and animated with so few desires, as soon as they engage in play, they become rapacious, impatient, noisy, and almost frantic with eagerness. Their furs, their domestic utensils, their clothes, their arms, are staked at play, and when all is lost, high as their sense of independence is, in a wild emotion of hope or despair, they will often risk their personal liberty upon a single bet. Among several tribes, such gaming parties are frequently made, and become their most agreeable entertainment at every great festival.

The same causes that contribute to render them fond of play, is the cause of drunkenness among them. It seems to have been one of the first exertions of the human ingenuity to discover some composition of an intoxicating quality; and there is hardly any nation so rude, or so destitute of invention, as not to have succeeded in this fatal research. The most barbarous of the American tribes have been so unfortunate as to attain this art; and even those, which are so deficient in knowledge, as not to be acquainted with

the

the method of giving an inebriating strength to liquors by fermentation, can accomplish the same by some other means.

It is customary with the American Indians, when their parents and other relations become old, or labour under any distemper which they have not art enough to cure, to put an end to their lives, in order to be relieved from the burden of tending and supporting them. The same hardships and difficulty of procuring subsistence, which prevent savages, in some cases, from rearing their children, prompt them to destroy the aged and infirm. The declining state of the one is as helpless as the infancy of the other; and the American thinks he does nothing more than his duty, in easing his father or friend of a burthensome life of pain and disease.

A hardness of heart and insensibility of feeling are remarkable in all savage nations. Their minds, roused only by strong emotions, are little susceptible of gentle, delicate, or tender affections. When any favour is done him, he neither feels gratitude, nor thinks of making any return. The high idea of independence among the Americans nourishes a sullen reserve, which keeps them at a distance from each other.

A savage,

A savage, frequently placed in situations of danger or distress, depending on no one but himself, and wrapped up in his own thoughts and schemes, is a serious and melancholy animal. The American, when not engaged in action, often sits whole days in one posture, without opening his lips. When they engage in war or the chace, they usually march in a line at some distance from each other, and do not exchange a single word. Even in their canoes, the same profound silence is observed; and nothing but intoxicating liquors or jollity attending their dances, can at any rate render them in the least conversable.

We may attribute the refined cunning, with which they form and execute their schemes, to the same causes. With the American Indians, war is a system of craft, in which they trust for success to stratagem more than to open force, and have their invention continually at work to circumvent and surprise their enemies. The people of the rude tribes of America are remarkable for their artifice and duplicity. The natives of Peru were employed above thirty years, in forming the plan of an insurrection, which took place under the vice-royalty of the Marquis de Villa Garcia; and though a great number of people

people of different ranks, were let into the
secret, yet not a syllable of it transpired
during all that period; no man betrayed
his trust, or by an unguarded look, or imprudent word, gave rise to any suspicion
of what was meditating.

However, let us not suppose that the
Americans were without their virtues,
among which fortitude and courage were
remarkably conspicuous. Accustomed as
the Indians are to continual alarms, they
grow familiar with danger; courage becomes an habitual virtue, resulting naturally from their situation, and strengthened by constant exertions. They are
naturally attached to the community of
which they are members. From the
nature of their political union, we should
be led to suppose this tie to be very
feeble; but each individual freely and
cheerfully undertakes the most perilous
service, when the community deems it
necessary. They have a fierce and deep-
rooted antipathy to the enemies of their
country, and that zeal for the honour
of their tribe, which prompts them to
brave danger in the pursuit of triumph,
and to endure the most exquisite tor-
ments, without a groan, that it may
not be dishonoured. Far from com-
plaining

plaining of their own situation, or viewing that of men in a more improved state with admiration or envy, they regard themselves as the standard of excellence, as being the best entitled, as well as the most perfectly qualified, to enjoy real happiness.

CHAP.

## CHAP. V.

AMBITION and avarice united to induce Velafquez to prepare for the conqueft of New Spain, fo that when Grijalva returned to Cuba, he found the armament deftined to attempt the conqueft of that rich country he had difcovered, almoft complete and ready to fail. Velafquez knew not whom to entruft with the command of this important expedition. Though he was of a moft afpiring ambition, and not deftitute of talents for government, he poffeffed neither fuch courage, nor fuch vigour and activity of mind, as to undertake in perfon the conduct of the armament he was preparing. He meanly wifhed to find fome perfon, who had bravery and abilities equal to the undertaking, but would attribute all the honour and glory to him. After fome time fearching for fuch a perfon, and finding that no man of abilities would fubmit to fuch difgraceful terms, he at laft appointed Fernando Cortes to the command. Cortes was a man of noble blood, but whofe family was of moderate fortune: he was a good foldier, and every way qualified for fuch an undertaking.

Though the governor had laid out considerable sums, and each adventurer had exhausted his stock, or strained his credit, the poverty of the preparation was such, as must astonish the present age, and bore no resemblance to an armament destined for the conquest of a great empire. The fleet consisted of eleven vessels, the largest of one hundred tons, which was dignified with the name of Admiral; three of seventy or eighty tons, and the rest small open barks. On board of these were 617 men; of which 508 belonged to the land-service, and 109 were seamen or artificers. As the use of fire-arms among the nations of Europe was hitherto confined to a few battalions of regular disciplined infantry, only thirteen soldiers were armed with muskets; thirty-two were cross-bow men, and the rest had swords and spears. They had only sixteen horses, and ten small field-pieces.

On the 10th of February, 1519, Cortes sailed with this small armament to attack a most powerful monarch. He touched first at Cozumal, then at Tabasco, and on the 2d of April arrived at St. Juan de Ulua in Mexico. As soon as they entered the harbour, a boat came off to them, to know what was the intention of their visit, and to offer them their assistance if needful. Cortes assured them, in respectful terms,

terms, which he did by means of an interpreter, that he approached their country with moſt friendly ſentiments, and came to propoſe matters of great importance to the welfare of their prince and his kingdom, which he would unfold more fully, in perſon, to the governor and the general. Next morning, without waiting for any anſwer, he landed his troops, his horſes, and artillery; and having choſen proper ground, began to erect huts for his men, and fortify his camp.

The Mexicans treated the Spaniards with the greateſt civility, but wiſhed to divert them from their intention of viſiting the capital, where the emperor Montezuma reſided. For this purpoſe, they commenced a negociation, by introducing a train of an hundred Indians loaded with preſents, ſent from Montezuma to Cortes. The magnificence of theſe were ſuch as became a great monarch, and far exceeded any idea the Spaniards had hitherto formed of his wealth. They were placed upon mats ſpread on the ground, in ſuch order as ſhewed them to the greateſt advantage. Cortes and his officers viewed with admiration the various manufactures of the country; cotton ſtuffs ſo fine, and of ſuch delicate texture, as to reſemble ſilks; pictures of animals, trees, and other natural objects, formed with feathers of different

different colours, difposed and mingled with fuch fkill and elegance, as to rival the works of the pencil in truth and beauty of imitation; but what more particularly attracted the attention of the Spaniards, was the amazing quantity of unwrought gold and filver, and the profufion of pearls and precious ftones, the produce of the country.

These rich prefents, inftead of inducing the Spaniards to quit Mexico, made them the more refolute to make a conqueft of it. Cortes infifted on vifiting the king in his capital, and declared he would not leave the ifland till that was granted. Of all the princes who had fwayed the Mexican fceptre, Montezuma was the moft haughty, violent, and impatient of controul. His fubjects viewed him with awe, and his enemies with terror. The former he governed with unrelenting rigour, and the latter he reduced to awe by the power of his arms. However, though his power and tyranny kept his fubjects and neighbours in awe, yet he wanted thofe qualities of mind, which were neceffary to intimidate and fubdue his new vifitors.

Montezuma, from the moment the Spaniards appeared on his coaft, difcovered fymptoms of timidity and embarraffment. Inftead of taking fuch refolutions as his power enabled him, he deliberated with an
anxiety

anxiety and hesitation that did not escape the notice of the meanest of his courtiers. He spent his time in fruitless negociations with the Spaniards, and thereby raised their courage and consequence.

In the mean time, Cortes was watching the opportunity to throw off all connections with Velasquez, whose natural jealousy had induced him to endeavour to deprive Cortes of the command of the expedition before he sailed. He got the confidence of the officers and soldiers, and, having assembled a council, he resigned the commission he had received from Velasquez, and was immediately chosen chief-justice and captain-general of the new colony.

Cortes owed much of his success to the Mexican gold, which he distributed with a liberal hand among both friends and opponents, and thereby brought all to be of one mind. Having thus settled every thing to the satisfaction of his army, by engaging it to join him in disclaiming any dependence on the governor of Cuba, he thought he might now venture to quit the camp, in which he had hitherto remained, and advance into the country. To this he was encouraged by an event no less fortunate than seasonable. He received a proffer of friendship from the cazique of Zimpoalla, a considerable town at no great distance. He found by their message,
that

that they were filled with such dread and hatred of Montezuma, that nothing could be more acceptable to them, than a prospect of deliverance from the oppressions under which they groaned. Cortes was highly delighted to find, that the great empire he intended to attack was not united, nor its sovereign beloved.

Some officers, whom Cortes had employed to survey the coast, having discovered a village about forty miles to the northward, which, as well on account of the fertility of the soil, as commodiousness of the harbour, seemed to be a more proper station for a settlement than that where he was encamped, he determined to remove thither; Zimpoalla lay in his way, where the cazique welcomed him in the manner he had reason to expect. He received Cortes with respect, almost approaching to adoration, and like one to whom he looked up as a deliverer. From the cazique he learned many particulars with respect to the character of Montezuma, whom he represented as a tyrant, haughty, cruel and suspicious. Cortes assured the cazique, that one great object of the Spaniards in visiting a country so remote from their own, was to redress grievances, and to relieve the oppressed.

Having taken his leave of the cazique, he continued his march to Quiabislan. The

The spot his officers had chosen as a proper situation, appeared so well to meet his approbation, that he immediately marked out ground for a town. The houses to be erected were only huts; but these were to be surrounded with fortifications, of sufficient strength to resist the assaults of an Indian army. Every one, even Cortes not excepted, gave an helping hand to the erecting of fortifications, so essential to the preservation of every individual of the colony. His next care was to form an alliance with the neighbouring kings, whom he taught to despise their emperor, by gradually inspiring them with an high opinion of the Spaniards, as beings of a superior order, and irresistible in arms.

Cortes perceiving that some of his men grew tired of their present pursuits, and had even formed the plan of making their escape to Cuba in one of the ships, saw no hopes of success, but in cutting off all possibility of retreat, and reducing his men to the necessity of adopting the same resolutions with which he himself was animated, either to conquer or perish. With this view he determined to destroy his fleet, and his address in persuading his followers to adopt his ideas, was not inferior to the boldness of the undertaking. With universal consent the ships were drawn ashore, and after stripping them of
their

their sails, rigging, iron work, and whatever else might be of use, they were broken in pieces. Thus, from an effort of magnanimity, to which there is nothing parallel in history, five hundred men voluntarily consented to be shut up in a hostile country, filled with powerful and unknown nations; and, having precluded every means of escape, left themselves without any resource but what their own perseverance and valour could procure them, and on which every thing now depended.

On the 16th of August, 1519, Cortes began his march from Zimpoalla, with five hundred men, fifteen horse, and six field pieces. The remainder of his troops, consisting chiefly of such as from age or infirmity were less fit for active service, he left as a garrison in Villa Rica, under the command of Escalante, an officer of merit, and warmly attached to the interest of Cortes.

The first war he engaged in was with the Hascalans, who advanced against him with numerous armies, and attacked him in various forms, with a degree of valour and perseverance, to which the Spaniards had seen nothing equal in the New World. The Hascalans, however, were at last glad to sue for peace, seeing their own people so dreadfully destroyed, while the Spaniards remained unhurt.

"If

"If (said they to the Spaniards) you are divinities of a cruel and savage nature, we present to you five slaves, that you may drink their blood and eat their flesh. If you are mild deities, accept an offer of incense and variegated plumes. If you are men, here is meat, and bread and fruit, to nourish you." As both parties were equally desirable of peace, matters were soon settled between them. The Hascalans acknowledged themselves as dependant on the crown of Castile; when Cortes took the republic under his protection, and promised to secure them against every attempt of injury or violence on their persons or property.

On the 13th of October, Cortes set out on his march for Mexico, accompanied by six thousand Hascalans; so that he now appeared at the head of something like a regular army. As the Spaniards descended from the mountains of Chalco, over which the road lay, the vast plain of Mexico gradually unfolded itself to their view. This prospect afforded one of the most striking and beautiful views on the face of the earth; when they beheld fertile and cultivated fields, stretching beyond the reach of the human eye; when they saw a lake resembling the sea in extent, encompassed with large towns, and beheld the capital city rising upon an island in the centre, adorned with its temples and turrets; the prospect so far surpassed their most sanguine expectations, that some believed the fanciful descriptions of romance were realized, and that its enchanted palaces and gilded domes were presented to their sight; others could hardly persuade themselves, that this wonderful sight was any thing more than a dream. As they proceeded their doubts were removed, but their amazement encreased.

Cortes was almost at the gates of the capital before Montezuma had determined, whether he should receive him as a friend, or oppose him as an enemy. On their arrival near the city, about a thousand persons, who bore marks of distinction, came out to meet them, dressed in mantles of fine cotton, and adorned with plumes. Each of these separately passed Cortes, and paid the most submissive obedience to him according to the mode of their country. They announced the approach of Montezuma himself, and his harbingers soon after came in sight. Two hundred persons in an uniform dress first appeared, ornamented with feathers, proceeding two and two, barefooted, and in profound silence, with their eyes fixed on the ground. A company of higher rank next followed, in their most sumptuous ornaments; in the midst of whom was Montezuma, in a

litter

litter richly ornamented with gold, and feathers of various colours. He was carried on the shoulders of four of his principal favourites, while others supported a canopy of curious workmanship over his head. Before him marched three officers with rods of gold in their hands, which they lifted up on high at certain intervals, when all the people immediately bowed their heads and hid their faces, as unworthy to look on so great a monarch. As soon as he approached, Cortes dismounted, advanced towards him with officious haste, and in a respectful posture. Montezuma immediately alighted from his chair, and leaning on the arms of two of his near relations, approached with a slow and stately step, his attendants covering the streets with cotton cloth, that he might not touch the ground. Cortes accosted him with profound reverence, after the European fashion; and Montezuma returned the salutation according to the mode of his country, by touching the earth with his hand, and then kissing it. Montezuma conducted Cortes to the quarters he had prepared for his reception, and immediately took leave of him with a politeness not unworthy of a court more refined. Nothing material passed at this first interview.

In the evening, Montezuma returned to visit his guests with the same pomp as in their first interview. He told Cortes, that from what he had heard and seen of him and his followers, he was convinced, that they were the very persons, whose appearance the Mexican traditions and prophecies taught them to expect, in order to reform their constitutions and laws; that he had accordingly received them, not as strangers, but as relations of the same blood and parentage, and desired that they might consider themselves as masters in his dominions, for both himself and his subjects should be ready to comply with their will, and even to prevent their wishes. The three subsequent days were employed in viewing the city; the appearance of which, so far superior in the order of its buildings, and the number of its inhabitants, to any place the Spaniards had beheld in America, filled them with wonder and surprise.

Though the novelty of these objects amused the Spaniards, yet they were not without their alarms on account of their safety. The allies of the Spaniards assured Cortes, that the Mexican priests had, in the name of the gods, counselled their sovereign to admit the Spaniards into the capital, that he might cut them off there at one blow with perfect security.

Cortes

Cortes very plainly perceived, that his deſtruction was intended; it was therefore neceſſary to extricate himſelf out of the difficulties, in which one bold ſtep had involved him, by venturing upon another ſtill bolder. The ſituation was trying, but his mind was equal to it; and, after revolving the matter with deep attention, he fixed upon a plan no leſs extraordinary than daring. He determined to ſeize Montezuma in his palace, and to carry him as a priſoner to the Spaniſh quarters. The plan being properly ſettled between Cortes and his officers, this powerful prince was ſeized by a few ſtrangers, in the midſt of his capital, at noon day, and carried off as a priſoner without oppoſition or bloodſhed. Hiſtory contains nothing parallel to this event, either with reſpect to the temerity of the attempt, or the ſucceſs of the execution; and were not all the circumſtances of this extraordinary tranſaction authenticated by the moſt unqueſtionable evidence, they would appear ſo wild and extravagant, as to go far beyond the bounds of reaſon and probability.

On the 4th of December, 1519, Qualcopoca, the ſon of Montezuma, and five of the principal officers who ſerved under him, were brought priſoners to the capital, formally tried by a Spaniſh court-

court-martial, and, though they had acted no other part than what became loyal subjects and brave men, they were condemned to be burnt alive, which was immediately put in execution. The rigour with which Cortes punished the unhappy persons, who first presumed to lay violent hands upon his followers, seems to have made all the impressions he desired. The spirit of Montezuma was not only overawed, but subdued. During six months that Cortes remained in Mexico, the Monarch continued in the Spanish quarters, with an appearance of an entire satisfaction and tranquillity, as if he had resided there, not from constraint, but through choice. His ministers and officers attended him as usual, he took cognizance of all affairs, and every order was issued in his name. The external aspect of government appearing the same, and all its ancient forms being scrupulously observed, the people were so little sensible of any change, that they obeyed the mandates of their monarch with the same submissive reverence as ever. Thus, by the fortunate temerity of Cortes in seizing Montezuma, the Spaniards at once secured to themselves more extensive authority in the Mexican empire, than it was possible to have acquired in a long course of time by open force; and they exercised more

absolute

abfolute fway in the name of another, than they could have done in their own.

Cortes, encouraged by fo many inftances of the monarch's tame fubmiffion to his will, ventured to put it to a proof ftill more trying. He urged Montezuma to acknowledge himfelf a vaffal of the king of Caftile, to hold his crown of him as fuperior, and to fubject his dominions to the payment of an annual tribute. With this requifition, the laft and moft humbling that can be made to one poffeffed of fovereign authority, Montezuma was fo obfequious as to comply. The act of fubmiffion and homage was executed with all the formalities the Spaniards were pleafed to dictate.

The next attempt Cortes made was to alter their religion, which had fuch an effect upon the Mexicans, that they determined to deftroy the Spaniards if they perfifted in it; and even Montezuma himfelf had expreffed his wifh to Cortes, that he would think of returning home.

While things continued in this critical fituation, Cortes, anxious about what was paft, uncertain with refpect to the future, and much oppreffed by the late declaration of the Mexicans, he received an account of fome fhips having appeared on the coaft. He idly imagined, that his meffengers were returned from Spain, and that the completion

pletion of all his hopes and wishes were at hand. However, a courier soon brought certain information, that the armament was fitted out by Velasquez, governor of Cuba, and, instead of bringing the aid they expected, threatened them with immediate destruction. This armament was commanded by Pamphilo de Narvaez.

Cortes was now greatly alarmed, as Narvaez seemed determined to ruin him, having received orders from Velasquez to seize him, and send him to Cuba in irons. Cortes at first attempted to treat with his enemies; but finding that impossible, he marched against them with an army infinitely inferior to theirs, and rushing upon them in the night, obtained a complete victory. Narvaez was wounded, taken prisoner, and put in irons.

This victory proved the more acceptable, as it was gained with little bloodshed, only two soldiers being killed on the side of Cortes, and two officers, with fifteen private men, of the adverse faction. Cortes treated the vanquished not like enemies, but as countrymen and friends, and offered to send them back immediately to Cuba, or to take them into his service, as partners in his fortune, on equal terms with his own soldiers. The greater part of them accepted the offer, and vied with each other in professions of fidelity

fidelity and attachment to a general, whose recent successes had given them such a striking proof of his abilities. Thus, by a series of events no less fortunate than uncommon, Cortes not only escaped from the destruction that seemed inevitable, but, when he had least reason to expect it, was placed at the head of a thousand resolute Spaniards.

While Cortes was engaged in this business, the Mexicans seized the opportunity of his absence to take up arms, to which they had been more particularly urged by the cruelty and treachery of Alvarado, whom Cortes had left in the city, in order to take care of the royal prisoner, and keep the natives in awe.

On the 24th of June, 1520, Cortes marched back to the city, and took quiet possession of his ancient station. However, being too much elated with his success, he neglected to visit Montezuma, and embittered the insult by expressions full of contempt for that unfortunate prince and his people. This being remoured about, they flew to arms in every quarter, and attacked the Spaniards in their fortifications. Though the artillery pointed against their numerous battalions, crowded together in narrow streets, swept off multitudes at every discharge, though every blow of the Spanish weapons fell with
mortal

mortal effect upon their naked bodies, the violence of the assault by no means abated. Fresh men rushed forward to occupy the places of the slain, and meeting with the same fate, were succeeded by others no less intrepid and eager for vengence. The utmost efforts and abilities of Cortes, seconded by the disciplined valour of his troops, were hardly sufficient to defend the fortifications of the Spaniards, into which the Mexicans had nearly forced their way.

Cortes was now willing to try what effect the sight of the emperor would have upon his subjects. He was accordingly brought on the ramparts, from whence he addressed the Mexicans, exhorting them to peaceable measures, which so enraged them, that he was soon wounded by two arrows, and the blow of a stone on his temples brought him to the ground. The Spaniards carried him to his apartments; but he was so broken and dejected by the severity of his fate, that he tore off the bandage from his wounds, and soon expired.

Soon after the death of Montezuma, Cortes found it absolutely necessary to abandon the city. He attempted his retreat by night, but the Mexicans, who had watched all his motions, fell upon him in his march, and destroyed nearly
one

one half of his army. All the artillery, ammunition, and baggage, were loſt, and only a very ſmall portion of the treaſure they had amaſſed was ſaved. Many of the ſoldiers, having ſo overloaded themſelves with bars of gold as rendered them unfit for action, and retarded their flight, fell ignominiouſly the victims of their own inconſiderate avarice.

Cortes directed his march towards a riſing ground at ſome little diſtance, and having fortunately diſcovered a temple ſituated on an eminence, he took poſſeſſion of it. He there found not only the ſhelter for which he wiſhed, but, what was no leſs wanted, ſome proviſions to refreſh his men. On leaving this place, they marched for ſix days with little reſpite, and under continual alarms, numerous bodies of the Mexicans hovering around them, and haraſſing them in front, rear, and flank, with great boldneſs. As the barren country through which they paſſed afforded hardly any proviſions, they were reduced to feed on berries, roots, and the ſtalks of green maize; and, at the very time that famine was depreſſing their ſpirits and waſting their ſtrength, their ſituation required the moſt vigurous and unremitting exertions of courage and activity. Amidſt theſe complicated diſtreſſes, one circumſtance ſupported and animated the Spaniards,

niards. Their commander sustained this sad reverse of fortune with unshaken magnanimity. His presence of mind never forsook him, his sagacity foresaw every event, and his vigilance provided for it. He was foremost in every danger, and endured every hardship with cheerfulness. His soldiers, though despairing themselves, continued to follow him without reluctance.

On the sixth day of their march, they reached the summit of an eminence, when a spacious valley opened to their view, covered with a vast army, extending as far as the eye could reach. The Mexicans, while with one body of their troops they harassed the Spaniards in their retreat, had assembled their principal force on the other side of the lake, and posted it in the plain of Otumba, through which they knew Cortes must pass. At the sight of this incredible multitude, which they could survey at once from the rising ground, the Spaniards were astonished, and even the boldest began to despair. Cortes, however, without allowing leisure for their fears to acquire strength by reflection, after reminding them, that nothing remained but to die or conquer, led them immediately to the charge. The Mexicans with unusual fortitude, waited their approach; but such was the superiority

riority of the Spanish arms and discipline, that the impression of this small body was irresistible, and whichever way its force was directed, it penetrated and dispersed the most numerous battalions. However, while these gave way in one quarter, a fresh supply of enemies advanced from another, and the Spaniards, though successful in every attack, were ready to sink under these repeated efforts, without seeing any end of their toil, or any hope of victory.

Cortes now observed, that the great standard of the empire, which was carried before the Mexican general, was advancing. He fortunately recollected to have heard, that on the fate of it depended the event of every battle. He therefore assembled a few of his bravest officers, whose horses were still capable of service, and placing himself at their head, pushed forwards towards the standard, with an impetuosity that bore down every thing before it. A chosen body of nobles, who guarded the standard, made some resistance, but were soon vanquished. Cortes, with a stroke of his lance, wounded the Mexican general, and threw him to the ground. One of the Spanish officers alighting, finished his life, and seized the imperial standard. The instant their leader fell, and their standard, to which all directed their eyes, was no

M 2 longer

longer to be seen, an universal panic struck the Mexicans, every ensign was lowered, each soldier threw away his weapons, and every one made the best of his way to the mountains. The Spaniards, who were not in a condition to pursue them, contented themselves with collecting the spoils of the field, which were so valuable, as to be some compensation for the wealth they had lost in the city of Mexico.

After this victory, Cortes dispatched an officer of confidence with four Ships of Narvaez's to Hispaniola and Jamaica, to engage adventurers, and to purchase horses, gunpowder, and other military stores. As he knew it would be in vain to attempt the reduction of Mexico, unless he could secure the command of the lake, he found means to procure materials for building twelve brigantines, so that they might be carried thither in pieces, ready to be put together, and launched, whenever he should want them.

While he was harassed and perplexed with the mutinous disposition of his troops, two ships arrived, with a supply of men and military stores, sent by the governor of Cuba, not to assist Cortes, but with a view to complete his ruin. His address, however, brought them over to his views. He now found his army reinforced with 180 Spaniards, and twenty horses.

Soon

Soon after this four Ships arrived at Vera Cruz from Hispaniola, with two hundred soldiers, eigthy horses, and two battering cannon, and a considerable supply of ammunition and arms.

On the 28th of April, 1521, all the Spanish troops, together with the auxiliary Indians, were drawn up on the banks of the canal; and with extraordinary military pomp, heightened and rendered more solemn by the celebration of the most sacred rights of religion, the brigantines were launched. Cortez now determined on making an attack on the city of Mexico. The brigantines no sooner appeared before the city, than the lake was covered with innumerable canoes, which made but a feeble resistance against these vessels, manned by Europeans. The brigantines, with the utmost ease, broke through their feeble opponents, overset many canoes, and dissipated the whole armament with such slaughter, as convinced the Mexicans, that it was not in their power to contend with the Spaniards on the watery element.

Cortes now determined to attack the city, and for this purpose he made all the wise preparations an able general could do; but, owing to his orders not being properly observed, he was at last repulsed, received some dangerous wounds, and would have been taken by the Mexicans, had

had not some Spanish officers rescued him at the expence of their lives. Forty Spaniards fell alive into the hands of the Mexicans, who sacrificed those unhappy victims, in the most cruel manner, to their god of war.

However unpromising an aspect matters wore at present, Cortes had a mind that rose above all difficulties. He soon found himself enabled to renew the attack on the city of Mexico, in which he proved so fortunate, that he took the emperor Guatimozin prisoner, who seemed worthy of a better fate. When the emperor was conducted to Cortes, he appeared neither with the sullen fierceness of a barbarian, nor with the dejection of a supplicant. "I have done (said he, addressing himself to the Spanish general) what became a monarch. I have defended my people to the last extremity. Nothing now remains but to die. Take this dagger, (laying his hand on one which Cortes wore) plant it in my breast, and put an end to a life, which can no longer be of use."

As soon as the fate of this unfortunate sovereign was known, the Mexicans ceased all resistance, and Cortes took possession of that small part of the capital, which had not been destroyed during the siege. Thus terminated the sige of Mexico, the most memorable event in the conquest of America.

America. It lasted twenty-five days, of which hardly one passed without some singular effort on the part of the besiegers or the besieged. The great abilities of Guatimozin, the number of his troops, the peculiar situation of his capital, so far counterbalanced the superiority of the Spaniards in arms and discipline, that they must have relinquished the enterprize, had they trusted for success to themselves alone; but Mexico was overturned by its own tyranny, and the jealousy of its neighbours.

The Spaniards were no sooner masters of the city, than they set about seeking for the profuse riches they expected it would produce; but they were herein sadly disappointed. The soldiers could collect only an inconsiderable booty amidst ruins and desolation, and this disappointment excited them almost to an open rebellion against Cortes. Arguments, entreaties, and promises, were employed in order to soothe them; but with so little effect, that Cortes, with a view to check this growing spirit of discontent, gave way to a deed, which stains the glory of all his great actions. The unhappy monarch, together with his chief favourite, were given up to be tortured, in order to force from them a discovery of the royal

treasures,

treasures, which it was supposed they had concealed. Guatimozin bore whatever the refined cruelty of his tormentors could inflict with the invincible fortitude of an american warrior. His fellow sufferer, sinking under the violence of his anguish, turned his sorrowful eyes towards his master, which seemed to implore his permission to reveal all he knew; but the high-spirited prince, darting on him a look of authority, mingled with scorn, checked him by asking, "Am I now reposing on a bed of flowers?" His favorite felt the reproach, persevered in his dutiful silence, and expired. Cortes was so much ashamed of this horrid scene, that he rescued the royal victim from the hands of his torturers, and thereby prolonged a life devoted to future miseries.

The fate of the capital, as both parties had conjectured, decided that of the empire, and the provinces submitted, one after another, to the conquerors. Cortes, being now more at leisure, began to form schemes of discovery, and to complete the original plan of Columbus, by finding a passage to the East Indies by that quarter of the world they were then in; but he did not then know that this scheme had been undertaken and accomplished.

Ferdinand Magellan, a Portuguese gentleman, on the 10th of August, 1519, sailed

sailed from Sevile with five Ships, and, after touching at the Canaries, stood directly South along the coast of America, and on the 12th of January, 1520, reached the river De la Plata. From hence he continued his course, after having conquered the mutinous disposition of his crew, and at length discovered, near the fifty-third degree of latitude, the mouth of a strait, into which he entered, in spite of the murmurs and remonstrances of the people under his commend. After sailing twenty days in that winding dangerous channel, to which he gave his own name, and where one of his ships deserted him, the great Southern Ocean opened to his view, when he shed tears of joy and gratitude for that happy discovery.

After enduring inexpressible hardships, from the want of provisions and other necessaries, on the 6th of March, 1521, they fell in with a cluster of small but fertile islands, which afforded them refreshments in such abundance, that their health was soon re-established. This extensive sea Magellan called the *Pacific Ocean*, which name it still bears. He afterwards discovered the Philippine islands, and was there killed by the barbarous natives.

John Sebastian del Cano prosecuted the expedition after the death of Magellan. After visiting many of the smaller islands, scattered in the eastern part of the Indian
Ocean,

Ocean, they touched at the great island of Borneo, and at length landed in Tidore, one of the Moluccas. He followed the course of the Portuguese by the Cape of Good Hope, and, after many disasters and sufferings, he arrived at St. Lucar on the 7th of September, 1522, having sailed round the globe in the space of three years and twenty-eight days.

But let us return to the transactions in New Spain. At the time that Cortes was acquiring such vast territories for his native country, and preparing the way for future conquests, it was his singular fate not only to be destitute of any commission or authority from the sovereign, whom he was serving with such successful zeal, but to be regarded as an undutiful and seditious subject. The court of Spain sent a person to supersede him, to seize his person, and confiscate his effects; but Cortes triumphed over all his enemies, and was appointed Captain-General, and Governor of New-Spain.

The jealousies and ingratitude of the court of Spain threw so many obstacles in the way of Cortes, that his government became very uneasy to him, and the court went so far as to send persons to enquire into his conduct, and to bring him to justice, should his interested judges find him guilty. He resolved, however, not to expose himself to the ignominy of a trial, a trial, in that country, which had been the scene of his triumphs; and, without waiting for the arrival of his judges, to repair directly to Castile, and commit himself and his cause to the justice and generosity of the King.

The Emperor Charles, having now nothing to apprehend from the designs of Cortes, received him at Court like a person, whom conscious innocence had brought into the presence of his master, and who was entitled, by the eminence of his services, to the highest marks of distinction and respect. The order of St. Jago, the title of Marquis del Valle de Guaxaca, and the grant of a vast territory in New Spain, were successively bestowed upon him.

Cortes returned to New Spain; but his power was so cramped, that he found himself in a very disagreable situation. He formed schemes for new discoveries, explored California, and surveyed the greater part of the gulf which separates it from New Spain. On his return to his government, he found himself surrounded with so many enemies, that he determined once more to seek for redress in his native country.

On his arrival in Old Spain, the Emperor behaved to him with cold civility, his ministers treated him sometimes with neglect, and sometimes with insolence.

His

His grievances received no redress, his claims were urged without effect, and several years passed in fruitless applications to ministers and judges: an occupation the most irksome and mortifying to a man of spirit. Cortes finished his mortal career on the second day of December, 1547, in the sixty-second year of his age, having experienced the same fate with that of all the persons who distinguished themselves in the discovery or conquest of the New World: envied by his cotemporaries, and ill requited by the courts he served, he has been admired and celebrated by succeeding ages.

*Remarkable Events recorded in this Chapter.*
1518 Cortes is sent by Velasquez to conquer New Spain.
1519 Lands his troops in New Spain.
Destroys his own fleet.
Sets out for Mexico with his little army.
1520 Montezuma acknowledges himself a vassal of Spain.
Death of the Emperor Montezuma.
1521 The conquest of all Mexico, followed by the taking of the city.
The Strait of Magellan discovered.
1522 Cortes appointed Captain-general and Governor of New Spain.
1536 Cortes discovers California.
1540 Returns home, and there dies.

CHAP. VI.

## CHAP. VI.

THE discovery of the Southern Ocean by Balboa excited a spirit of adventure in the colonies of Darien and Panama, who sighed after the imaginary wealth of those unknown regions. Several armaments were fitted out in 1523, in order to explore and take possession of the countries to the East of Panama, but under the conduct of leaders, whose talents and resources were unequal to the attempt. They proved unsuccessful, and thereby damped the ardour of others.

Three persons settled in Panama, whose names were Francisco Pizarro, Diego de Almagro, and Hernando Luque, resolved to attempt the discovery of Peru, notwithstanding the ill success of former adventurers. These three men were destined to overturn one of the most extensive empires on the face of the earth; though Pizarro was a bastard, with very little education; Almagro, a foundling; and Luque, a priest and schoolmaster at Panama.

Each engaged to employ his whole fortune in this adventure. Pizarro, being the poorest of the three, undertook the department of the greatest fatigue and danger, and to command in person the armament destined for the discovery. Almagro was to conduct the supplies of provisions and reinforcements of troops, of which Pizarro might stand in need. Luque was to remain at Panama to negociate with the governor, and superintend whatever was carrying on for the general good. As the spirit of enthusiasm uniformly accompanied that of adventure in the New World, and by that strange union both acquired an encrease of force, this confederacy, formed by ambition and avarice, was confirmed by the most solemn act of religion. Luque celebrated mass, divided a consecrated host into three, and reserving one part to himself, gave the other two to his associates, of which they partook, and thus, in the name of the Prince of Peace, ratified a contract, of which plunder and bloodshed were the principal objects in view.

On the 14th of November, 1525, Pizarro set sail from Panama with a single vessel, of small burthen, and 112 men. His voyage, however, was attended with great difficulties and hardships. After remaining five months in the island of Gorgona, noted for the most unhealthy climate in that region of America, a vessel arrived from Panama. This transported them with such joy, that all their former sufferings were forgotten. Their hopes revived,

revived, and Pizarro found little difficulty to induce not only his own followers, but also the crew of the veffel from Panama, to refume his former fcheme with no lefs ardour. Inftead of returning to Panama, they ftood towards the South-eaft, and, more fortunate in this than in any of their paft efforts, on the twentieth day after departure from Gorgona, they difcovered the coaft of Peru.

After touching at feveral villages on the coaft, they landed at Tumbez, a place of fome note, about three degrees fouth of the line, diftinguifhed for its ftately temple, and a palace of the Incas, or fovereigns of the country. There the Spaniards feafted their eyes with the firft view of the opulence and civilization of the Peruvian empire. They beheld a country fully peopled, and cultivated with an appearance of regular induftry; the natives decently cloathed, and poffeffed of ingenuity fo far furpaffing the other inhabitants of the New World, as to have the ufe of tame and domeftic animals. But what chiefly attracted their notice, was fuch a fhow of gold and filver, not only in the ornaments of their perfons and temples, but in feveral veffels and utenfils for common ufe, formed of thofe precious metals, as left no room to doubt that they abounded with profufion in the country. Pizarro and his companions now seemed to have attained the completion of their most sanguine hopes, and fancied that all their wishes and dreams of rich domains, and inexhaustible treasures, would soon be realized.

Pizarro, having explored the country as far as it was necessary to ascertain the importance of the discovery, procured from the inhabitants some of their *Llamas*, or tame cattle, to which the Spaniards gave the name of sheep; some vessels of gold and silver, as well as some specimens of their other works of ingenuity; and two young men, whom he proposed to instruct in the Castilian language, that they might serve as interpreters in the expedition he meditated. With these he arrived at Panama, towards the close of the third year from the time of his departure thence. No adventurer of the age suffered hardships or encountered dangers, which equal those to which he was exposed during this long period.

On their arrival at Panama, Pizarro could not prevail on the governor to assist him in the conquest of Peru; his associates therefore sent him to Spain to negociate, where he managed matters more to his own interest than to theirs. On the 26th of July, 1528, Pizarro was appointed governor, captain-general, and adelantado of the countries he had difcovered, and hoped to conquer, with fupreme authority, civil as well as military: thus he fecured to himfelf whatever his boundlefs ambition could defire.

After all the efforts of Pizarro and his affociates, three fmall veffels, with 180 foldiers, 36 of whom were horfemen, compofed the whole of the armament. With this contemptible force, in February, 1531, Pizarro did not hefitate to fail to invade a great empire.

He no fooner landed in Peru, than he began hoftilities, by which imprudent conduct his followers were expofed to famine, fatigue, and difeafes of various kinds. However, they at length reached the province of Coaque; and having furprized the principal fettlement of the natives, they feized there, veffels and ornaments of gold and filver to the amount of thirty thoufand pefos, with other booty of fuch value, as difpelled all their fears, and infpired the moft defponding with fanguine hopes.

The dominions of the fovereigns of Peru, at the time that the Spaniards invaded them, extended in length, from north to fouth, above fifteen hundred miles along the Pacific Ocean. Its breadth, from eaft to weft, was much lefs confiderable, being uniformly bounded by the vast ridge of the Andes, stretching from its one extremity to the other.

Pizarro, soon after his landing in Peru, discovered that a civil war was carrying on in that country. By these means he was permitted to pursue his operations unmolested, and advanced to the centre of a great empire, before one effort of its power was exerted to stop his career. The first complete information the Spaniards received of this war, was by messengers from Huascar, one of the contending parties, sent to Pizarro, in order to solicit his aid against his opponent Atahualpa. Pizarro at once perceived the importance of this intelligence, and foresaw so clearly all the advantages, which might be derived from this divided state of the kingdom he had invaded, that, without waiting for the reinforcements he expected from Panama, he determined to push forward, while intestine discord put it out of the power of the Peruvians to attack him with their whole force, and while by taking part, as circumstances should incline him, with one of the competitors, he might be enabled with greater ease to crush them both.

Strange as it may appear, Pizarro marched into the heart of the country attended by his followers, consisting only of 62 horsemen, and 102 foot soldiers, of whom

whom twenty were armed with crossbows, and three with muskets. Pizarro, in the couse of his march, received an embassador from the inca of Caramalca, who brought him very valuable presents from that prince, accompanied with a proffer of his alliance. Pizarro, according to the usual artifice of his countrymen in America, promised every thing, without meaning to fulful any thing but what his interest directed. In consequence of these declarations, the Spaniards were permitted to march where they pleased.

On entering Caxamalca, Pizarro took possession of a large court, on each side of which was a house, which the Spanish historians calls a palace of the Inca, and on the other a temple of the Sun, the whole surrounded with a strong rampart or wall of earth. When he had posted his troops in this advantageous situation, and had seen what profusion of riches the Inca possessed, Pizarro treacherously seized on his person, during the interview to which the monarch had invited him. While the Inca was engaged in conference with the Spaniards, Pizarro gave the signal of assault. At once the martial musick struck up, the cannon and muskets began to fire, the horse sallied out fiercely to the charge, and the infantry rushed on sword in hand. The Peruvians, astonished

at

the irresistible impression of the cavalry, fled with universal consternation in every quarter, without attempting either to annoy the enemy, or to defend themselves. Pizarro, at the head of his followers, advanced directly towards the Inca; and, though his nobles crowded around him with officious zeal, and fell in numbers at his feet, while they vied one with another in sacrificing their own lives, that they might cover the sacred person of their king, the Spaniards soon penetrated to the royal seat, and Pizarro, seizing the Inca by the arm, dragged him to the ground, and carried him as a prisoner to his quarters. The fate of the monarch precipitated the flight of his followers. The Spaniards every where pursued them, and with a deliberate and unrelenting barbarity, continued to slaughter the wretched Peruvians, who never attempted to resist. The carnage did not cease till the close of the day put an end to it, when above four thousand Peruvians lay dead on the spot. Not a single Spaniard fell, nor was any one wounded but Pizarro himself, whose hand was slightly hurt.

The plunder the Spaniards acquired on this massacre, was far beyond every thing they

they had formed in their minds of the wealth of Peru, and they were so transported with the value of the acquisition, as well as the greatness of their success, that they passed the night in those extravagant exultations natural to indigent adventurers on so sudden a change in their affairs.

The captive monarch could at first hardly believe what he saw to be real, and the dejection into which he sunk was in proportion to the height of grandeur from which he had fallen. However, the Inca soon discovered the ruling passion of the Spaniards, and by applying to that, made an attempt to recover his liberty. He offered as a ransom what astonished the Spaniards, even after all they now knew concerning the opulence of his kingdom. The apartment in which he was confined was twenty-two feet in length, and sixteen in breadth; he undertook to fill it with vessels of gold as high as he could reach. Pizarro eagerly closed with this tempting proposal, and a line was drawn upon the wall of the chamber, to mark the stipulated height to which the treasure was to reach.

As fast as the gold was brought in, it was melted down, except some pieces of curious fabric, which were reserved as a present for the emperor. After setting apart

apart the fifth due to the crown, and a hundred thousand pesos as a donative to the soldiers, who were just arrived with Almagro, there remained 1,528,500 pesos to Pizarro and his followers. The festival of St. James, (July 25, 1513) the patron saint of Spain, was the day chosen for the partition of this vast sum. Though assembled to divide the spoils of an innocent people, procured by deceit, extortion, and cruelty, the transaction began with a solemn invocation of the name of God, as if they could have expected the guidance of heaven in distributing those wages of iniquity. In this division, about 8000 pesos, at that time not inferior in effective value to as many pounds sterling of the present century, fell to the share of each horseman, and half that sum to each foot soldier. Pizarro and his officers received their dividends in proportion to their superior station.

The Inca having thus fulfilled his engagement, demanded his release; but the treachery of the Spaniards induced them, instead of setting him at liberty, to put a period to his life. He was tried, and condemned to be burnt alive. At last, the unfortunate prince consented to receive baptism, and was therefore indulged with being strangled at the stake.

Pizarro,

Pizarro, having by these cruel proceedings established his authority in Caxamalca, no longer hesitated to advance towards Cuzco; and, having received considerable reinforcements, he could venture, with little danger, to penetrate into the interior part of the country. The Peruvians had assembled some large bodies of troops to oppose his progress, and several fierce encounters happened; but they terminated like all the actions in America: a few Spaniards were killed or wounded, and the natives were put to flight with incredible slaughter. At length Pizarro forced his way to Cuzco, and took quiet possession of the capital. The riches found there, even after all the natives had carried off and concealed, either from a superstitious veneration for the ornaments of their temples, or out of hatred to their rapacious conquerors, exceeded in value what had been received as the Inca's ransom. However, as Pizarro's forces were now more numerous, the common soldiers did not receive so much as they expected, which proved a disappointment to their rapacity.

After all these conquests, Pizarro set out for his native country, and arrived in Spain in 1534. The immense quantities of gold and silver which he imported, filled the kingdom with astonishment.

Pizarro was received by the Emperor with the attention due to the bearer of a present so rich, as to exceed any idea the Spaniards had formed concerning the value of their acquisitions in America, even after they had been ten years masters of Mexico. Pizarro was admitted into the order of St. Jago, and, after getting his authority confirmed with new powers and privileges, he set out on his return to Peru, accompanied by many persons of higher rank than had yet served in that country. Almagro received the honours he had so long desired: the title of Adelantado, or governor, was conferred upon him, with jurisdiction over two hundred leagues of country, stretching beyond the southern limits of the province allotted to Pizarro.

On his arrival at Peru, he found Almagro in arms opposing his interest, and endeavouring to do himself justice for the treacherous conduct of Pizarro, who had engrossed to himself all the honours and emoluments, which ought to have been divided with his associate. However, matters were soon accommodated between them. Their new agreement was confirmed with the same sacred solemnities as the first, and observed with as little fidelity.

Cuzco, the capital city of the Incas, was situated in a corner of the empire, above

above four hundred miles from the sea, and much further from Quito, a province of whose value he had formed an high idea. No other settlement of the Peruvians was so considerable as to merit the name of a town, or to allure the Spaniards to fix their residence in it. Pizarro, in marching through the country, had been struck with the beauty and fertility of the valley of Rimac, one of the most extensive and best cultivated in Peru. There, on the banks of a small river, of the same name with the vale which it waters and enriches, at the distance of six miles from Callao, the most commodious harbour in the Pacific Ocean, he founded a city, which he destined to be the capital of his government. On the 18th of January, 1535, he gave it the name of Cindad de los Reyes, either from the circumstance of having laid the first stone, at that season when the church celebrates the festival of the Three Kings, or, as is more probable, in honour of Juana and Charles, the sovereigns of Castile. This name it still retains among the Spaniards in all legal and formal deeds, but it is better known to foreigners by that of *Lima*, a corruption of the ancient appellation of the valley in which it is situated. Under his inspection, the buildings advanced with such rapidity, that it soon

O      assumed

assumed the form of a city, which, by a magnificent palace that he erected for himself, and by the stately houses built by several of his officers, gave a strong proof of the grandeur it was at last to acquire.

Almagro, as agreed on between him and Pizarro, set out for Chili; but on his march, he met with so many hardships and difficulties, that many of his men died with fatigue. They no sooner entered on the fertile plains of Chili, than they met with new difficulties to encounter. They there found a race of men very different from the people of Peru, intrepid, hardy, independant, and in their bodily constitution, as well as vigour of spirit, nearly resembling the warlike tribes in North America. Though filled with wonder at the first appearance of the Spaniards, and still more astonished at the operation of their cavalry, and the effects of their fire-arms, the Chilese soon recovered so far from their surprize, as not only to defend themselves with obstinacy, but to attack their new enemies with more determined fierceness than any American nation had hitherto discovered. The Spaniards, however, continued to penetrate into the country, and collected some considerable quantities of gold, when they were recalled to Peru by an unexpected event.

The

The Inca of Peru, having observed the inconsiderate security of the Spaniards in dispersing their troops, and that only a handful of soldiers remained in Cuzco, thought that the happy period was at length come for vindicating his own rights, for avenging the wrongs of his country, and extirpating its oppressors. The Inca, who was the prisoner of Pizarro, obtained permission from him to attend a great festival, which was to be celebrated a few leagues from the capital. Under pretext of that solemnity, the great men of the empire were assembled. As soon as the Inca joined them, the standard of war was erected, and, in a short time, all the fighting men, from the confines of Quito to the frontiers of Chili, were in arms. Many Spaniards, living securely on the settlements allotted them, were massacred. Several detachments, as they marched carelessly through a country which seemed to be tamely submissive to their dominion, were cut off to a man. The Spanish writers assert, that the Peruvian army amounted to 200,000 men, and with this powerful army, and their Inca at the head of it, they laid siege to Cuzco. During nine months they carried on the siege with incessant ardour, and in various forms. The Inca, in spite of the valour of the Spaniards, recovered possession of one half of his capital; and, in their various efforts to drive him out of it, Pizarro loſt one of his brothers, and ſome other perſons of note.

Almagro arrived at Cuzco in a critical moment. The Inca at firſt endeavoured to gain the friendſhip of Almagro; but after many fruitleſs overtures, deſpairing of any cordial union with a Spaniard, he attacked him by ſurprize with a numerous body of choſen troops. However, the Spaniſh diſcipline and valour maintained their uſual ſuperiority. The Peruvians were repulſed with ſuch ſlaughter, that a great part of their army diſperſed, and Almagro proceeded to the gates of Cuzco without oppoſition.

The Spaniards had no ſooner got rid of their Peruvian enemies, than they began to quarrel among themſelves, and the flame at laſt burſt out into a civil war. Though countrymen and friends, the ſubjects of the ſame ſovereign, each with the royal ſtandard diſplayed; and though they beheld the mountains that ſurrounded the plain in which they were drawn up, covered with a vaſt multitude of Indians, aſſembled to enjoy the ſpectacle of their mutual carnage, and prepared to attack whatever party remained maſter of the field; ſo fell and implacable was the rancour which had taken poſſeſſion of every
breaſt,

breaſt, that not one pacific council, not a ſingle overture towards accommodation, proceeded from either ſide. Almagro was defeated and taken, tried by the Pizarros as guilty of treaſon, and condemned and executed, in 1538.

However rapid the progreſs of the Spaniards had been in South America ſince Pizarro landed in Peru, their avidity of dominion was not yet ſatisfied. The officers to whom Ferdinand Pizarro gave the command of different detachments, penetrated into ſeveral new provinces, and though ſome of them were expoſed to great hardſhips in the cold and barren regions of the Andes, and others ſuffered diſtreſs not inferior amidſt the woods and marſhes of the plains, they made diſcoveries and conqueſts which not only extended their knowledge of the country, but added conſiderably to the territories of Spain in the New World. Pedro de Valdivia reaſſumed Amagro's ſcheme of invading Chili, and notwithſtanding the fortitude of the natives in defending their poſſeſſions, made ſuch progreſs in the conqueſt of the country, that he founded the city of St. Jago, and gave a beginning to the eſtabliſhment of the Spaniſh dominions in that province.

Gonzalo Pizarro, whom his brother Franciſco had made governor of Quito, had

had entrusted one of his confidential officers, named Orellana, with an expedition on discoveries, appointing a proper place where they were to meet; but this young officer began to fancy himself independent, and, transported with the predominant passion of the age, formed schemes of distinguishing himself as a discoverer, and treacherously abandoned his friend and employer.

It is impossible to describe the consternation of Pizarro, when he did not find the bark at the confluence of the Napo and Maragnon, where he had ordered Orellana to wait for him; but that treacherous servant, after having made some discoveries, got back to Spain, and there magnified his wonderful exploits. In the mean time, Pizarro was twelve hundred miles from Quito; and, in that long march back to their capital, the Spaniards encountered hardships greater than those they had endured in their progress outward, without the alluring hopes that then soothed and animated them under their sufferings. Hunger compelled them to feed on roots and berries, to eat all their dogs and horses, to devour the most loathsome reptiles, and even to knaw the leather of their saddles and sword belts. Four thousand Indians, and two hundred and ten Spaniards perished in this wild and disasterous expedition, which continued near two years. Those that got back to Quito were naked like savages, and so emaciated with famine, or worn out with fatigue, that they had more the appearance of spectres than men.

Gonzalo Pizarro was not much more happy on his arrival at his government of Quito, where he found every thing in a state little short of open rebellion against his brother Francisco. The young Almagro, after the execution of his father, never lost sight of taking revenge of Pizarro. He possessed all the qualities which captivate the affection of soldiers; he was of a graceful appearance, dexterous at all martial excercises, bold, open and generous, he seemed to be formed for command; and as his father, conscious of his own inferiority from the total want of education, had been extremely attentive to have him instructed in every science becoming a gentleman, the accomplishments he had acquired heightened the respect of his followers, as they gave him distinction and eminence among illiterate adventurers. In this young man the Almagrians found a point of union which they wanted, and looking up to him as their head, were ready to undertake any thing to promote his interest. Their affection for Almagro was not the only incitement,

citement, being urged on by their own
distresses. Many of them, destitute of
common necessaries, and weary of loiter-
ing away life a burden to their chief, or
to such of their associates as had saved
some remnant of their fortune from pillage
and confiscation, sighed for an occasion
to exert their activity and courage, and
began to deliberate how they might be
avenged on the author of all their misery.
Juan de Harrada, an officer of great abilities, who had the charge of Almagro's
education, took the direction of their
consultations, with all the zeal which
this connection inspired, and with all the
authority which the ascendency that he
was known to have over the mind of his
pupil gave him.

On Sunday, the 6th of June, 1541, at
midnight, the season of tranquillity and
repose in all sultry climates, Harrada, at
the head of eighteen of the most determined conspirators, sallied out of Almagro's
house in complete armour, and drawing
their swords, hastily advanced towards the
governor's house. Their associates, warned
of their motions by a signal, were in arms
at different stations to support them.
Though Pizarro was usually surrounded
by such a numerous train of attendants,
as suited the magnificence of the most
opulent subject of the age in which he
lived,

lived, yet he was juſt riſen from table, and moſt of his domeſtics had retired to their own apartments, ſo that the conſpirators paſſed through the two outward courts of the palace unobſerved. They were at the bottom of the ſtaircaſe, before a page in waiting could give the alarm to his maſter, who was converſing with a few friends in a large hall. The governor, whoſe ſteady mind no form of danger could alter, ſtarting up, called for arms, and commanded Franciſco de Chaves to make faſt the door; but that officer, who did not retain ſo much preſence of mind as to obey this prudent order, running to the top of the ſtaircaſe, wildly aſked the conſpirators what they meant, and whither they were going. Inſtead of anſwering, they ſtabbed him to the heart, and burſt into the hall. Some of the perſons who were there threw themſelves from the windows, others attempted to fly, and a few, drawing their ſwords, followed their leader into an inner apartment. The conſpirators, animated with having the object of their vengeance now in view, ruſhed forward after them. Pizarro, with no other arms than his ſword and buckler, defended the entry, and ſupported by his half brother Alcantara, and his little knot of friends, he maintained the unequal conteſt with intrepidity worthy of his paſt exploits,

exploits, and with the vigour of a youthful combatant, "Courage, (cried he) companions, we are yet enow to make those traitors repent of their audacity." But the armour of the conspirators protected them, while every thrust they made took effect. Alcantara fell dead at his brother's feet, and his other defenders were mortally wounded. The governor, unable any longer to parry the many weapons furiously aimed at him, received a deadly thrust full in his throat, funk to the ground, and expired.

As soon as Pizarro was killed, the assassins ran out into the streets, and waving their bloody swords, proclaimed the death of the tyrant. About two hundred of their associates having joined them, they conducted young Almagro in solemn procession through the city, and assembling the magistrates and principal citizens, compelled them to acknowledge him as lawful successor to his father in his government.

Matters were not properly settled, when the arrival of Vaco de Castro, who assumed the title of governor, threw every thing again into fresh confusion. Castro and Almagro both took the field. The former, knowing his strength to be far superior to that of the enemy, he was impatient to determine the contest by a battle. Nor
did

*Pizarro assassinated in his Palace.*

p. 151.

did the followers of Almagro, who had no hopes of obtaining a pardon for a crime so atrocious as the murder of the governor, decline that mode of decision.

On the 16th of September, 1542, they met at Chupaz, about two hundred miles from Cuzco, and fought with all the fierce animosity inspired by the violence of civil rage, the rancour of private enmity, the eagerness of revenge, and the last efforts of despair. Victory, after remaining long doubtful, declared at last for Vaco de Castro. The carnage was great in proportion to the number of combatants. Of fourteen hundred men, the total amount of the armies on both sides, five hundred lay dead on the field, and the number of the wounded was still greater. Of the prisoners, Castro condemned some to death, others were banished Peru, and Almagro being taken, was publickly beheaded.

The feelings of the emperor were exceedingly hurt at the recital of so many actions shocking to humanity. He perceived, that relieving the Indians from oppression was but one step towards rendering his possessions in the New World a valuable acquisition, and would be of little avail, unless he could circumscribe the power and usurpations of his own subjects there. With this view, he formed

a body

a body of laws, containing many salutary appointments with respect to the constitution and powers of the supreme council of the Indies; concerning the station and jurisdiction of the royal audiences in different parts of America; and the order of government, both ecclesiastical and civil.

Notwithstanding these regulations, Peru was hastening to the highest pitch of anarchy and confusion. Castro however, by his wise and prudent measures, for some time averted the storm. A viceroy was sent over by the emperor, and, soon afer his arrival in Peru, he was first imprisoned, and, after obtaining his liberty, and raising an army to support his authority, was slain in battle. In this critical situation, the emperor sent over Pedro de la Gasca as president of Peru, who, by his moderation and good management, might have done great things, had not Gonzalo Pizarro, supported by a strong party, assumed the government of Peru. Gasca, perceiving that force must be employed in order to accomplish the purpose of his mission, collected troops in all quarters.

On the 9th of April, 1548, as the two parties moved forward to the charge, they exhibited a very singular appearance. In that of Pizarro, composed of men enriched
with

with the spoils of the most opulent country in America, every officer, and almost all the private men, were clothed in stuffs of silk or brocade, embroidered with gold and silver; and their horses, their arms, their standards, were adorned with all the pride of military pomp. That of Gasca, though not so splendid, exhibited what was no less striking. He himself, accompanied by the archbiship of Lima, the bishops of Quito and Cuzco, and a great number of ecclesiastics, marching along the lines, blessed the men, and encouraged them to a resolute discharge of their duty, which could not fail that day of restoring Peru to peace and tranquility.

When both armies were just ready to engage, several of Pizarro's principal officers set spurs to their horses, and went over to Gasca, and many others silently slipped away. Pizarro, seeing all irretrievably lost, cried out in amazement to a few officers, who still faithfully adhered to him, " What remains for us to do?" —" Let us rush (replied one of them) upon the enemy's firmest battalion, and die like Romans." Pizarro, dejected with such a reverse of fortune, had not spirit to follow this soldierly counsel, and, with a tameness disgraceful to his former fame, he surrendered to one of Gasca's officers. Gasca, happy in this bloodless victory,

P did

did not stain it with cruelty. Pizarro, and a small number of the most distinguished or notorious offenders, were capitally punished. Pizarro was beheaded on the day after he surrendered. He submitted to his fate with a composed dignity, and seemed desirous to atone by repentance for the crimes he had committed.

Pizarro was no sooner dead, than the malcontents in every quarter of Peru laid down their arms, and tranquillity was soon restored. Gasca then endeavoured to find employment for the mutinous soldiers who had laid down their arms, which he did by engaging them in the conquest of Chili. In order to reward his own soldiers, he made a division of the country among them, without reserving the smallest portion to himself.

Gasca, having now accomplished every object of his mission, and longing to return again to a private station, committed the government of Peru to the court of audience, and set out for Spain on the first of February, 1550.

There had been no remittance of the the royal revenue for four years, owing to the distracted state of the country. Gasca, however, on his return to Spain, carried with him 1,300,000 pesos of public money, which the prudence and good order of administration enabled him to
save;

save, after paying all the expences of the war. He was received in his native country with univerſal admiration and eſteem for his abilities and his virtues, both which were highly conſpicuous. Without army or fleet, or public funds; with a train ſo ſimple, that only three thouſand ducats were expended in equipping him, he ſet out to oppoſe a formidable rebellion. But the praiſe beſtowed on his abilities were exceeded by that which his virtues merited. After reſiding in a country where wealth preſented allurements, which had ſeduced every perſon who had hitherto poſſeſſed power there, he retired from the trying ſtation with integrity, not only untainted but unſuſpected. After diſtributing among his countrymen poſſeſſions of greater extent and value than had ever been in the diſpoſal of a ſubject in any age or nation, he himſelf remained in his original ſtate of poverty; and at the very time, when he brought ſuch a large recruit to the royal treaſury, he was obliged to apply by petition for a ſmall ſum to diſcharge ſome petty debts, which he had contracted during the courſe of his ſervices. Charles was not inſenſible to ſuch diſintereſted merit. Gaſca was received by him with the moſt diſtinguiſhed marks of eſteem, and being promoted to the biſhopric of Palencia, he paſſed the remainder of his days in the tranquillity of retirement, respected by his country, honoured by his sovereign, and beloved by all.

*Memorable Events recorded in this Chapter.*

1526 Pizarro discovers Peru.
1528 He is appointed governor of the newly-discovered countries.
1532 Massacre of the Peruvians by the Spaniards.
1533 The Inca of Caxamalca tried, condemned, and executed.
1534 Pizarro arrives in Spain.
1535 On his return to Peru, he builds Lima.
    Chili invaded by Almagro.
1536 Siege of Cuzco.
1538 Almagro tried, condemned, and executed.
1541 Pizarro assassinated in his palace.
1546 Pedro de la Gasca appointed President of Peru.
1548 He suppresses the rebellion in Peru.
1550 Returns to Spain, and is made Bishop of Palencia.

## CONCLUSION.

HAVING now taken a review of the conquest of the two great empires of Mexico and Peru, very little more seems worthy of notice in the History of South America, than to mention a few circumstances relative to their political institutions and national manners.

According to the account of the Mexicans themselves, their empire was not of long continuance. They relate, that their country was originally possessed, rather than peopled, by small independent tribes, whose manners and mode of life resembled those of the rudest savages in South America. About a period corresponding to the beginning of the tenth century in the Christian æra, several tribes moved in successive migrations from unknown regions towards the north and north-west, and settled in different provinces of Anahuac, the ancient name of New Spain. These, more civilized than the original inhabitants, began to form them to the arts of social life. At length, towards the commencement of the thirteenth century, the Mexicans, a people more polished than any of the former, advanced from the borders of the Californian gulf, and took possession of the plains adjacent to a great lake near the centre of the country. After residing there about fifty years they founded a town, since distinguished by the name of *Mexico*, which from humble beginnings soon grew to be the most considerable city in the New World. The Mexicans, long after they were established in their new possessions, continued, like other martial tribes in America, unacquainted with regal dominion;

dominion; and were governed in peace, and conducted in war, by such as were entitled to pre-eminence by their wisdom or their valour. Among them, as in other states, whose power and territories become extensive, the supreme authority centered at last in a single person; and when the Spaniards under Cortes invaded the country, Montezuma was the ninth monarch in order, who had swayed the Mexican sceptre, not by hereditary right, but by election. Such is the traditional tale of the Mexicans concerning the progress of their own empire, which, according to this account, must have been but of short duration.

While the jurisdiction of the Mexican monarchs was limited, it is probable that much ostentation was not exercised; but as their authority became more extensive, the splendour of their government encreased. It was in this last state the Spaniards beheld it, and struck with the appearance of Montezuma's court, they describe its pomp at great length, and with much admiration. The number of his attendants, the order, the silence, and the reverence with which they served him; the vast extent of his royal mansion, the variety of apartments allotted to different officers, and the ostentation with which his grandeur was displayed whenever he permitted his subjects to behold him, seem to resemble the magnificence of the ancient monarchies in Asia, rather than the simplicity of the infant states in the New World.

The Mexicans, like the rude tribes among them, were incessantly engaged in war, and the motives that prompted them to hostilities seem to have been the same. They fought in order to gratify their vengeance, by shedding the blood of their enemies. In battle, they were chiefly intent on taking prisoners, and it was by the number of these that they estimated the glory of victory. No captives were ever ransomed or spared: all were sacrificed without mercy, and their flesh devoured with the same barbarous joy as among the fiercest savages. On some occasions, it rose to even wilder excesses. Their principal warriors covered themselves with the skins of the unhappy victims, and danced about the streets, boasting of their own valour, and exulting over their enemies.

Their funeral rites were no less bloody than those of the most savage tribes. On the death of any distinguished personage, especially of the emperor, several of his attendants were chosen to accompany him to the other world, and these unfortunate victims were put to death without mercy, and buried in the same tomb.

Though the agriculture of the Mexicans was more extensive than that of the roving tribes, who trusted chiefly to their bow for food, it seems not to have supplied them with such subsistence as men require when engaged in efforts of active industry. The Spaniards appear not to have been struck with any superiority of the Mexicans over the other people of America in bodily vigour. Both, according to their observation, were of such a feeble frame as to be unable to endure fatigue, and the strength of one Spaniard exceeded that of several Indians. This they imputed to their scanty diet, on poor fare, sufficient to preserve life, but not to give firmness to the constitution.

In Mexico, though the disposition of the houses was somewhat orderly, yet the structure of the greater part of them was mean. Nor does the fabric of their temples, and other public edifices, appear to have been such as entitled them to the high praises bestowed upon them by many Spanish authors. The great temple of Mexico, the most famous in New Spain, which has been represented as a magnificent building, raised to such a height, that the ascent to it was by a staircase of an hundred and fourteen steps, was a solid mass of earth of a square form, faced partly with stone. Its base on each side extended ninety feet, and decreasing gradually as it advanced in height, it terminated in a quadrangle of about thirty feet, where were placed a shrine of the deity, and two altars on which the victims were sacrificed. Greater skill and ingenuity were displayed, if we may believe the Spanish historians, in the houses of the emperor, and in those of the principal nobility. There some elegance of design was visible, and a commodious arrangement of the apartments was attended to; but if buildings corresponding to such descriptions had ever existed in the Mexican cities, it is probable that some remains of them would still be visible. As only two centuries and a half have elapsed since the conquest of New Spain, it seems altogether incredible, that in a period so short every vestige of this boasted elegance and grandeur should have disappeared.

The Mexicans have been represented, perhaps, more barbarous than they really were; their religious tenets, and the rites of their worship, are described as wild and cruel in an extreme degree. The aspect of superstition in

Mexico

Mexico was gloomy and frightful; its divinities were cloathed with terror, and delighted in vengeance. They were exhibited to the people under deteſtable forms, which created horror. The figures of ſerpents, tygers, and other deſtructive animals, decorated their temples. Feaſts, mortifications, and penances, all rigid, and many of them excruciating to an extreme degree, were the means employed to appeaſe the wrath of their gods, and the Mexicans never approached their altars without ſprinkling them with blood drawn from their own bodies; but of all offerings, human ſacrifices were deemed the moſt acceptable.

The empire of *Peru* boaſts of an higher antiquity than that of Mexico. According to the traditionary accounts collected by the Spaniards, it had ſubſiſted four hundred years under twelve ſucceſſive monarchs; but the knowledge of their ancient ſtory, which the Peruvians could communicate to their conquerors, muſt have been both imperfect and uncertain. Like the other American nations, they were totally unacquainted with the art of writing, and deſtitute of the only means, by which the memory of paſt tranſactions can be preſerved with any degree of accuracy.

The authority of the Inca was unlimited and abſolute, in the moſt extenſive meaning of the words. Whenever the decrees of a prince are conſidered as the commands of the divinity, it is not only an act of rebellion, but of impiety, to diſpute or oppoſe his will. Obedience becomes a duty of religion; and as it would be profane to controul a monarch under the guidance of heaven, and preſumptuous to adviſe

him,

him, nothing remains but to submit with implicit respect. This must necessarily be the effect of every government established on pretensions of intercourse with superior powers. Such accordingly was the blind submission which the Peruvians yielded to their sovereign.

The Incas of Peru were immensely rich in gold and silver, long before they knew any thing of the rich silver mines of Potosi, which were accidentally discovered in the year 1545, by an Indian, as he was clambering up the mountains, in pursuit of a Llama which had strayed from his flock. Soon after the mines of Sacotecas in New Spain, little inferior to the other in value, were opened. From that time successive discoveries have been made in both colonies, and silver mines are now so numerous, that the working of them, and of some few mines of gold in the province of Tierra Firmé, and the new kingdom of Granada, has become the capital occupation of the Spaniards, and is reduced into a system no less complicated than interesting.

To return: the wars, in which the Incas engaged, were carried on with a spirit very different from those of other American nations. They fought not, like savages, to destroy and exterminate, or, like the Mexicans, to glut bloodthirsty divinities with human sacrifices. They conquered in order to reclaim and civilize the vanquished, and to infuse the knowledge of their own institutions and arts. Prisoners seem not to have been exposed to the insults and tortures, which were their lot in every other part of the New World. The Incas took the people whom they subdued under their protection, and admitted

p. 166.

Slaves at Work in the Silver Mines of Peru.

mitted them to a participation of all the advantages enjoyed by their original subjects.

In Peru, agriculture, the art of primary necessity in social life, was more extensive, and carried on with greater skill, than in any other part of America. The Spaniards, in their progress through the country, were so fully supplied with provisions of every kind, that in the relation of their adventures we meet with few of those dismal scenes of distress, occasioned by famine, in which the conquerors of Mexico were so often involved. The quantity of soil under cultivation was not left to the discretion of individuals, but regulated by public authority, in proportion to the exigencies of the community. Even the calamity of an unfruitful season was but little felt; for the product of the lands confecrated to the Sun, as well as those set apart for the Incas, being deposited in the public store-houses, it there remained as a stated provision for times of scarcity.

The ingenuity of the Peruvians was also conspicuous in the construction of their houses and public buildings. In the extensive plains, which stretch along the Pacific Ocean, where the sky is perpetually serene, and the climate mild, their houses were very properly built only of slight materials; but in the higher regions, where rain falls, where the vicissitudes of seasons are known, and their rigour felt, houses were constructed with greater solidity. They were generally of a square form, the walls about eight feet high, built with bricks hardened in the Sun, without any windows, and the door low and strait. Simple as these structures were, and rude as the materials may seem to be, of which they

were

were formed, they were so durable, that many of them still subsist in different parts of Peru, long after every monument, that might have conveyed to us any idea of the domestic state of the other American nations, has vanished from the face of the earth. It was in the temples consecrated to the Sun, and in the buildings destined for the residence of their monarchs, that the Peruvians displayed the utmost extent of their art and contrivance. The descriptions of them by some of the Spanish writers, who had an opportunity of contemplating them, while, in some measure entire, might have appeared highly exaggerated, if the ruins which still remain, did not vouch the truth of their relations.

The unwarlike Spirit of the Peruvians was the most remarkable, as well as the most fatal defect in their character. The greater part of the rude nations of America opposed their invaders with undaunted ferocity, though with little conduct or success. The Mexicans maintained the struggle in defence of their liberties with such persevering fortitude, that it was with difficulty they triumphed over them. Peru was subdued at once, and almost without resistance; and the most favourable opportunities of regaining their freedom, and of crushing their oppressors, were lost through the timidity of the people.

THE END.

www.ingramcontent.com/pod-product-compliance
Lightning Source LLC
Chambersburg PA
CBHW032142160426
43197CB00008B/751